"Please, papa! Please, papa!"
My grandfather was horrified to hear the
pleading of five-year-old Frank.
The sound of blows striking someone
again and again followed, along with my
brother's wild yells and sobbing.
Grandpa grabbed open the door and
there stood my father beating my
brother with a stick. My grandfather
grabbed my dad's arm and, in his frenzy,
my father almost knocked the old man
over.
"I'm teaching this young man to smile
when I tell nim to!"

I Was a Battered Child

RUTH
ELIZABETH
BAIRD

LIVING BOOKS
Tyndale House Publishers, Inc.
Wheaton, Illinois

NOTE: Some names in
this book have been
changed to protect
identities. In a few
instances the time and
place have been
varied slightly.

Library of Congress
Catalog Card
Number 79-66816
ISBN, 0-8423-1878-X, paper
Copyright © 1980 by
Ruth Elizabeth Baird
All rights reserved
First printing,
May 1980
Printed in the United
States of America

APPRECIATION

My deep gratitude
to God who healed
my painful memories.
Also my heartfelt
thanks to those who
cared, prayed, and
loved me when I
needed them through
the years.

CONTENTS

1 Hollow Years   9

2 Frank   22

3 A Touch of
   Tenderness   28

4 Heartbreak   35

5 Student Days   48

6 Nightmare   54

7 "There Is No
   Hope!"   60

8 On the Edge   65

9 Road to Peace   71

10 Circle of
   Prayer   81

11 Victory   87

12 "Put Away
   Lying"   90

13 Fight Against
   Jealousy   96

14 Answer to
   Gossip   102

15 Side Effects   110

   Epilogue   123

ONE
Hollow
Years

We were never called battered children, the
four of us. I was the only girl in our family
among three brothers, one younger and two
older. My elder brother always lived with my
grandparents. The term "battered child"
had not been coined when we were small—but
battered we were in body and spirit, for as
long as I can recall.

I never loved myself when I was young. I
thought I was junk. Inside I felt hollow. Part of
the reason for my feeling of aching inadequacy
was that we were never commended or praised
in our family. In larger measure it was because
of the brutality of my father.

I could have endured the physical clobbering
from him if he'd given me love or affirmation
—even a pat on the shoulder to let me know I was
approved of and appreciated. But like so
many parents, my dad had no idea of how to be

a loving father. He didn't know how to provide sustained and supportive attention, or training and supervision, along with consistent discipline.

Although my mother loved us children with an unconditional love, she was timid. Whenever my father was emotionally upset she feared for our safety, what he might do to us. She was always afraid he'd lose his temper and get fired from his job, as he so often did. Besides all this, she always worried about his wasting money on anything that took his fancy. All of us were concerned about his getting into an argument with anyone.

Like all children everywhere, my brothers and I longed for love, assurance, and security. Because my father's emotions went up and down, we lived in uncertainty, apprehension, and fear. We each had a serious inferiority complex. It was as if we were bent down before we were fully grown.

My two brothers never married and I left home when I was sixteen. The hurt and harm we children suffered at the hand of my dad stayed with us until . . .

The until is why this book is being written.

One afternoon when I was six years old my brothers and I were quarreling. I called one of them a sap. My dad, sitting in the next room, heard all we said. To hear me make this passing remark triggered his quick temper. We had no idea he was getting irritated. We had no warning of trouble.

Suddenly he rushed in and grabbed me. I was trapped, terrified. I felt needles of fear. I started quivering and trembling until I was shaking all over with fright. My teeth were chattering, but I never said a word. I knew I mustn't do anything to make my father any madder.

He snatched me into the hallway, slamming doors behind him. His eyes bulged. Holding me by my arm, he raised the big switch. The more he hit me the madder he became and the harder the blows. All his tension and inner turmoil came out at the end of his hand. He channeled his combative instincts, his frustration, onto us children. With every whack I saw stars. The pain was intense. It was as if every strike cut at least an inch into the flesh of my back and legs. My every breath was a gasp, as I tried to get enough air to keep screaming.

The welts and bruises took days to disappear. Mother consoled and comforted me as best she could with ointment and soothing words. She knew how enraged my dad became when he attacked any of us children so she never risked trying to stop him once he started in on us. There seemed to be nothing she could do once he began, but she did work out a system with me.

"When dad is mad," she cautioned, "hurry and stand behind me."

Sometimes she protected me by holding me tightly in her arms, which always kept my father from walloping me. Even in his worst outbursts, none of us ever knew him to hit her.

In times of distress and anxiety, my dad

reacted like a wounded animal: he was dangerous and unpredictable. Any incident, however insignificant or harmless, might cause him to explode at us. As little children, we were convenient targets. We couldn't defend ourselves. We couldn't fight back. So, whenever he felt like it, he wreaked his vengeance on his youngsters.

With such a father, we children lived under constant tension. I wanted to protect us from my father but I wasn't smart enough or big enough.

He followed the savage pattern of generation after generation before him.

No one helped my dad understand why he lashed out at us. The words we dreaded most from him were, "I'm out of fix." This was a dire warning that trouble was certain to erupt. "Fix" had no connection with drugs or narcotics, but meant rather that he was unhappy, impatient, out of sorts.

Early memories can be uncertain, yet too many of my memories have a sting to them. I don't remember much about the logging camp in Louisiana where I was born, but I do recall a screened porch where we played. Soon we went to live at another logging camp. But my first clear recollections are when my dad tried another occupation. When I was four years old we moved to a big alfalfa ranch in west Texas. This was the first of more moves than I care to count, thanks to my father's restless ways and volatile temper.

I remember the long dusty drive across the desert land and how glad we children were when we came rattling up to what looked like a green oasis. This was our new home. The small house assigned to my family did not interest us youngsters after the long confining ride. Instead my younger brother and I raced out to wade in the irrigation water that lay like a shining sheet over the front yard of our new home. Alkali in the water scalded our skin and we soon came crying back to the house. That night our feet felt as if they were on fire.

That introduction was only the first of a series of horrors. After that move to west Texas I can't recall ever feeling entirely safe or completely happy as a child. Our ranch home had no indoor plumbing, and it was on one of our first trips to the outhouse that my mother and I spied a snake coiled at the corner of our small wooden porch. A rattlesnake. My mother was terrified. My father killed it.

Just across the road from our scraggly green lawn, the desert began. It was a vast, windswept waste of sand, sagebrush, and mesquite.

"Children, don't ever wander there," my mother warned. "You might get lost and not find your way home again."

When I shuddered at that thought, my older brother, a sparkling-eyed, mischievous rascal, saw his chance for fun. He filled me with wild tales of the dread creatures he said waited in the desert—or in the dark—to pounce on children, particularly little girls. On nights when the coyotes howled in the distance, I pulled the covers up over my head to try and shut out their piercing wail.

Of course there were happy times too. I rode bareback on one of our horses, grasping my arms tightly around the mare's neck as she galloped over the ranch. At Christmas time my aunts sent me lovely dolls. One year my mother wanted to save an especially beautiful one for me to have when I was older. But, willful child that I was, I persuaded my brother to write to my aunt, who told my mother to let me play with that pretty doll right then. Thus it was short-lived.

On Saturdays we drove the six miles into the small town of Grandview, where we'd park on the main street and shop and visit with other ranch families. Part of the afternoon we'd sit in our car and criticize and pass judgment on all who passed by.

On Sundays we drove in to church. My dad often stood outside to talk with other men, until the service was over. Those Sundays were part social, too, and when the presiding elder came to visit our congregation, we had big dinners in the afternoon out under the trees. Long tables groaned with fried chicken and all the good food the women prepared.

Driving homeward I always listened carefully to the criticism my parents mouthed about the preacher and especially about his wife and children. We also devoured the latest gossip about other church members.

At home we children liked to wander out and look at the irrigation canal that flowed between fields not far from our house. One day we three youngsters were standing on the muddy bank, gazing with awe at the six-foot-wide stream gurgling along. Suddenly my dad was there. He laughed a hollow crackling laugh, then picked up my three-year-old brother and flung him into the canal. The water closed over his head. Then he bobbed up and clutched at the slimy banks with his tiny fists.

While my older brother and I screamed hysterically, my father stood with his hands on his hips and laughed uproariously. "Best way to teach him to swim," he said.

Mother came running and without a word waded into the water fully clothed. Picking up my choking, terrified little brother, she clutched him to her and carried him into the house.

MY DAD

My father was of Welsh background, the youngest child and the pet of his father, who died when he was only three years old. A year later his mother remarried. The new stepfather not only resented the child, but abused and mistreated him. At that time no one thought of the personality consequences of such treatment. No doubt my dad needed discipline because his older sisters and brothers, along with his parents, had petted and spoiled him. They told him he was gifted with everything a man could have—looks, personality, ability—and that the world should recognize this fact and act accordingly. They neglected to tell him that he had responsibility, that much is expected from one to whom much is given.

No doubt during his childhood my dad had temper tantrums when he didn't get his own way. As an adult, when this happened, it made him so mad that he either sulked at his disappointing attempts and failures or erupted like a volcano. He tried to believe he was a king, until circumstances forced him to realize he was an ordinary person. Instead of accepting his limitations and dealing with them, he reacted with violence. While the family tried to eke out a living on parched Missouri soil, if there was only one egg, my father would get it. He hated to study at school, so he quit in the fourth grade.

He was a tall, well-set man with ruddy cheeks. He had dark, wavy hair, and a glint in his eyes. At first sight he charmed any stranger he met. He held his head high. With his shoulders squared and a proud smile on his lips, he looked like an English lord.

My father never had any close male friends, possibly because he didn't know how to build friendships with men he wanted to know better. He refused to be friends with those he could get. Yet he held a fascination for women all his life long; affairs fulfilled his ego-craving. In the many communities where we lived, I can always recall the various places where my father's lady friends lived.

One of his associates called my father "pure, unadulterated cussed." Although he rarely went to church, if there was a discussion, my dad took over. Occasionally he would attend some special series. On seeing him, people would nod toward my dad. "Church can't do anybody any good when you see who goes there," they'd say, shaking their heads. He was a turbulent enigma of a man.

One summer he went to work at a logging camp in the Missouri Ozarks. Everything about lumbering fascinated him. He had an uncanny ability. He could walk through a forest, measure the girth of a few of the standing timber, count how many trees were growing in a specified area, and figure how many board feet of lumber that stand would cut. Such an ability would have been invaluable to a large lumber company if he had been able to get along with the other workers. But my father would not submit to any man, or to God.

I was an adult before I learned one secret of my dad's personality problems. It may have been a basis for some of his unpleasant actions and his difficulty in maintaining relationships with others. It might also account in part for the constant battle within himself.

My dad told me that one evening when he was twelve years old he had gone alone to a tent revival meeting in their little country town. The preacher urged all those present to turn their lives over to God by accepting Christ as Savior. My father said he walked out of that meeting all torn up inside, trying to decide what to do. As he trudged along he was in such anguish that he lay down in the grass beside the

road and rolled back and forth in an agony
of indecision. He was in torment as he fought
with himself.

Then at last the war was over.

Dad stood up, shook his fist toward the night
sky in a gesture of defiance, and yelled aloud,
"I'll live my own life, God. I'll get along without
you!"

That week one of his brothers went up to that
same tent altar. And what a difference it made in
the two of them. My uncle's children had a
secure, stable life with a gentle father.

When he turned thirty years old, my dad
decided to settle down. He promptly fell in love
with the talented daughter of one of the finest
families in Carthage, Missouri. She was
beautiful and charming. My father took her
home from the school where she taught. As they
rode along he talked as if he were conferring
a favor on her when he told her, "I'm going to
marry you."

"Oh, no, you're not!" she retorted. "Let me out
right here."

My dad confided to me that he'd loved my aunt
all his life. Because he was determined to
be a part of this outstanding family, my father
turned around and married the elder sister,
who became my mother.

MY MOTHER

With my father six feet tall, my mother seemed
shorter than her barely five-foot height. She
was a gentle person who made you want to

protect and shelter her. She had straight black
hair and a face like an aristocratic pixie.
Her eyes were wide and wondering like a child's,
because she had a handicap. She was hard
of hearing. In defense at missing part of what was
said, she developed an attitude of not caring,
of being self-contained. None but a few ever
knew that her favorite Bible verse, which she
repeated practically every day, was: "Great peace
have they who love thy law: and nothing
shall offend them" (Psalm 119:165). She needed
those words because there was scarcely a
day when she wasn't offended. People are unkind
to the deaf.

Although she seemed phlegmatic, her active,
eager mind kept track of everything she was able
to hear. Later she would ask someone what
words she'd missed. At an early age I became my
mother's "ears." I could practically repeat
an entire afternoon's conversation and she could
understand me clearly when I put my lips up
to her good ear.

As the eldest, with four younger sisters and
one brother, my mother could have been in
the center of their merriment. Instead she spent
a great deal of time with my grandfather,
who was a medical doctor. She worked in his
office and even accompanied him on his
house calls. She early found the joy of reading
books and magazines. She was a private person.

My mother went along to church with her
family because that's what they all did on
Sunday. She wanted to go to heaven because
that's where the others planned to go. She asked

little of life, and life gave her no more than she requested. That is, until she was thirty-two years old, the year she married. Then she got more than she expected.

Along with other young people, my dad was often a guest in my grandparents' home. He and my mother said hello time and again, so he knew how serene she was. Maybe because of the constant churning inside him, he longed for the peace she expressed in her calm, quiet manner. Whatever it was that triggered his decision, only he knows; but the week after my aunt turned him down, my father called on my mother and started dating her.

This time my dad was more subtle, but one evening he cautiously told my mother, "I'd like to marry you sometime." Mother said she's still surprised at her answer. (Some of the farmers, even older ones, had asked my grandfather, "Could I please have your oldest daughter's hand?" My mother was merely amused by their proposals.) When my father started talking about marriage, mother explained to me, "I was so dumbfounded that such a dashing, handsome young man would ask me that I answered with the same words he'd used. I told him, 'I'd like to marry you sometime, too.' So we were engaged and my family went into a whirlwind of activity to give me the kind of wedding they thought the oldest girl should have. Not at all the kind of quiet ceremony I would have preferred."

Those 300 guests who attended my parents' dazzling wedding never guessed how catastrophic the wedding night would be for the new bride. My father spent that first evening telling her about his conquests with former girl friends. Only pride kept my mother from rushing back to her parents' home. She never forgave my dad. War was declared that night, and my mother became more and more of a recluse. My father, who loved people, found his pleasure away from home in a lifetime series of extramarital affairs.

TWO
Frank

Few situations are sadder for a mother than to have her first child removed from her care. Imagine what it's like if the little one is being abused and mistreated. That's what happened in our family the year before I came into the world. My mother grieved all her life for her son who lived far away.

When Frank, their first child, was born, my father resented the new baby taking center stage and demanding so much of my mother's time. He reacted against him by poking him, pushing and shoving him, tickling him unmercifully, and even slapping and beating him.

Frank was a serious, sensitive child. In contrast, my next brother, two years younger, was a brilliant and adorable package of fun. From babyhood on, he used all his wiles to charm everyone. In order to protect himself from my dad's tantrums, he often blamed others for his naughtiness.

Once when our family—my mother, father, and two older brothers—were visiting my grandparents in Missouri, my dad and Frank had serious trouble. My grandfather came into his house one day and was horrified to hear five-year-old Frank pleading, "Please, Papa! Please, Papa!"

Then followed the sound of blows striking someone again and again, along with my brother's wild yells and sobbing. Grandpa grabbed open the door and there stood my father beating my brother with a stick. My grandfather grabbed my dad's arm and, in his frenzy, my father almost knocked the old man over. But the brutal flogging stopped.

"I'm teaching this young man to smile when I tell him to," was the only explanation my dad gave.

My brother had welts and bruises all over his back. The next day when Frank spilled his milk at the table, my father hit both sides of his head hard enough, it seemed, to break his eardrums. Grandma and Grandpa were in anguish. My mother wept with them. They talked far into the night and prayed a lot during the remainder of my parents' visit. It was already October and getting cold.

Then the afternoon before my folks were to leave, Frank took sick. My dad had to get back to work, but that night their son was worse. My mother was frantic, realizing that he couldn't possibly travel. How could they go without him? But would a sick child be able to ride over 1,200 miles and stand such a journey?

At last it was decided that Frank should stay with his grandparents. My mother wept as she said goodbye to her older son, hugging and kissing him again and again. My parents promised to be back the next spring to get him, but I put in my appearance and they couldn't travel. Two years later my younger brother came along. By the time we got back to Missouri, Frank was doing so well in school that Grandma and Grandpa begged for him to be allowed to finish out that year.

My mother again hated to leave her son behind, but my father didn't seem to mind. Anyway, we moved so often that three children were all they could squeeze into our car or that we could pay for on the train.

On our rare visits, my grandparents always managed to have some big project as a reason why Frank couldn't leave just then—a Boy Scout event, a band concert. There would be no such opportunity in the logging camp where we lived.

Each time when we left without him, Mother was silent on the drive home. She kept dabbing at her eyes. For a few days after we reached our house, she was like a robot.

Through all his growing-up years, Frank never visited us even once. I used to sit and dream of my absent brother. When things were bad, as they so often seemed to be, I'd yearn for him. I'd think, "If only he were here he could make everything right again." But he wasn't there and he never would be. My heart ached and longed for the sound of his voice, so many miles from us.

Occasionally my mother would mention Frank's name. She'd have a faraway look in her eyes and would give a long sigh. Then usually she'd hurry out of the room to be by herself. She couldn't spend much time thinking about Frank, though. There were still three of us to try to protect from my father.

The year Frank was fourteen, we went back to Missouri for a visit. One afternoon, thinking no one else was at home, my father started berating my mother. "Don't suggest anything to me," he yelled. "I'll live my own life."

That moment all four of us children entered the back door. As we came into the living room, Frank rose to his full height and shouted back at our dad, "Stop talking to Mother like that!"

For a moment my father seemed frozen with surprise. His mouth fell open in amazement that his young son, who was small for his age and whom he barely knew, would defy him. Frank didn't notice the look of anger on my dad's face. Suddenly my father clenched his fists shoulder high. Then, spreading his arms, he lunged at my brother, grabbed him by the throat, and started choking him.

My two brothers and I ran screaming out the front door just as a man walked past on the sidewalk. This stranger spun around and hurried back to us. We all talked at once, but somehow this passerby understood what was going on inside the house. He dashed in and pulled my dad away from Frank just as the youth was beginning to lose consciousness. Frank was rushed out of the house and hidden until our family left town.

My parents didn't see their eldest son again for nine years. By that time he'd grown to be a handsome six-footer with flawless skin and wavy brown hair. His deep-set blue eyes showed the compassion that only suffering brings.

That year he decided to surprise my mother and father by visiting them. Since my mother's hearing was even worse than when she was younger, my folks didn't have a telephone.

Frank, straight as a ramrod and impeccably dressed, walked up onto their front porch. Finding the front door unlocked, he stepped inside and saw my mother sitting in an easy chair. He crossed over, bent down, and kissed her lightly on the cheek.

Although this occasion was a dream come true for Frank, it was a moment of alarm and fright for my mother. She jumped to her feet and hurriedly pushed herself against the wall, never taking her eyes off my brother. She stood there trembling. In a terrified voice that could barely be heard, she gasped, "Dad, who *is* this man?"

My brother's head drooped and his shoulders slouched. He quickly reassured her, "I'm sorry I frightened you, Mother. I'm Frank. I'm your son, Frank."

"You're what?" my mother asked in

amazement, taking a step toward him.

"I'm your son, Mother. I'm Frank," he repeated and they were in each other's arms.

The atmosphere changed. She pulled him down beside her on the davenport and held his hand. "Tell me about yourself," she urged. His arm was around her shoulders.

Meanwhile my father had shaken Frank's hand and seated himself across the room from them.

For two hours they visited and then Frank walked the block with my mother to the company store and helped carry back the groceries. That evening my mother prepared her finest meal for her son. Since she was a marvelous cook, it was a banquet.

My father kept his distance most of the time during the week Frank was there. Neither mentioned what took place the last time they had seen each other.

But best of all for Mother, Frank had grown to be the kind of man she hoped he would be.

THREE
A Touch of Tenderness

During my growing-up years, the idea of a loving
heavenly Father sounded like a distortion
to me. My idea of God was a hazy, far-off force
whom I feared. God had no connection with
the emptiness of my life. I was uncertain,
apprehensive, and unhappy.

I can remember only one time when my dad
put his arms around me. I was small and we were
sitting near some other parents with their
children. When that father held his youngsters
on his lap, my father motioned me to him
and set me on his knee. It was strange and
unnatural. But even today a haunting description
of God for me is that of his "everlasting arms."

During those early years it wasn't only
that I was afraid of my dad for myself, but I feared
what he might do to one of my brothers.
Because he felt so inadequate himself, he wanted
his children to excel at everything, especially

school. If there was one thing my dad seemed to worship, it was education. Once my twelve-year-old brother, who usually made grades in the nineties, came home with a sixty-two in math. My dad glanced at the report card, then looked hard at my brother a moment. Then he grabbed his son by his shoulder and thigh, and raised him chest-high ready to dash him onto the floor. I covered my eyes in horror.

Mother cried out and Dad let his son drop with a sickening thud. From that moment I vowed I'd keep as far away from my father as possible.

A letter came inviting my dad to work for a logging company near Savannah, Georgia. He left the next day, leaving my mother to pack everything and follow him with us three children.

It was fun living there—with the magnolias and oysters—but pretty soon my father lost that job and we were back in Missouri again with my grandparents.

While we were living there I had one of the happiest six weeks of my entire childhood. My parents were separated at this time, because Dad had moved in with a woman whose husband was supposedly on a merchant ship going around the world. Dad always felt safe from entanglements, being married, and he always chose married women for his extramarital attachments. It came as a surprise, therefore, when this woman not only wanted to marry him, but she wanted his two youngest children. That meant me, eight years old, and my brother, who was six. I didn't understand it, but my young brother and I were guarded all the time from my dad. We were walked to school and called for again in the afternoon.

Those six weeks I was loved and cherished and felt appreciated for the first time in my life. I'd always wanted my mother to say she was proud of me and thought I was important. Here they were all saying it without words and the heart language was beautiful! Best of all, we were safe.

Dad hadn't intended to get seriously involved so he calmly solved the problem for himself by moving to a logging camp in Washington state. Two of my mother's sisters worked in the office there. As soon as he earned enough money he sent for us and we followed him out west.

When we arrived, our new home wasn't finished, so Mother and we three children moved in with my two aunts. They had crystal goblets that shook when we ran and other fancies that rattled. We were warned to keep quiet and still, but it was hard since it rained so much and we were indoors.

When I did something wrong one day, Mother's patience came unglued and she promised me a spanking when we moved into our own home. She threatened me again and again, but she never touched me. By the time we finally arrived at our new place I had a total of nine punishments coming to me.

Of course I dreaded moving, and the first night I cried myself to sleep. Nothing happened that day or the next. Every evening I'd cry in relief at not being punished that day. I'd fear what was surely going to happen tomorrow.

Finally my mother realized that something was wrong and I was relieved to tell her about it. Instead of disciplining me or limiting my privileges in some way, however, she only said, "You've suffered enough. We'll both forget about it." I didn't deserve my father's brutality in times past, but now I didn't deserve my mother's forgiveness. Because she failed to spank me, I realized I could misbehave and get by with it. I copied my father in arguing and being rebellious, so my mother just gave up on me.

That kind of permissiveness, however, made me feel more rejected. I wished with all my heart that my mother and father would share in my dilemmas and problems. I wanted to tell them about my trouble in getting along with other people.

Mistreatment of children seems almost catching in some families. Once when I was ten I begged my mother to let me go swimming with my brothers who went to a river close by. The water, which had melted from the snow-covered mountains, was ice cold. I intended to get used to the chill a little at a time, but my older brother decided otherwise.

Suddenly he grabbed me by my hands. One of his friends grabbed my feet, and together they threw me into a deep part of the Snoqualmie River. I screamed and coughed and sputtered as I surfaced, but I went under a second time before they believed I couldn't swim and pulled me out.

God provided a touch of tenderness in my life in the persons of my two aunts.

As a young woman, my Aunt Virginia had been engaged to a Baptist minister who went to France as an army chaplain. He died aboard his ship returning to the United States. I was the daughter she never had and as a child I used to worry about loving her more than I loved my own mother. Whenever possible, I went to their home. After we moved to other communities, I visited them in the summer, sometimes for as long as six weeks.

My aunts, however, were of the "no compliment" school. My efforts were minimized and I was always warned, "Never speak well of yourself; let others praise you." Whatever I accomplished, I was urged only to keep it up or do better if I could. I must have brought them pleasure, but they never said that they were proud of me. Like my mother and father, they were following the patterns their parents before them used.

I was seared and scarred by verbal attacks when I was not successful. My emotional needs were not satisfied. I was never commended. I recall making a cake for company, but the cake fell in the middle and it was a joke for months. Another time, I cleaned the house as a surprise and the first comment was, "Why didn't you put the candlesticks back on the mantel?"

I didn't know it then, but I know now that I *was* loved. My physical needs were met. The company store would always order anything we needed. But nothing could make up for the lack of a good relationship with my father.

Although she lived out her faith by a series of "dos" and "don'ts," my mother told me she had trusted Jesus when she was ten. She knew she belonged to him. In one camp she joined the church along with my older brother. When the minister asked if he could add my father's name, mother answered "yes." This preacher then asked if there were any others in the family he could add to the membership roster. He put my name down. I was nine at the time, but he didn't say anything to me personally. I had never heard that God had a plan for my life, and I had no idea about trusting him to save me. No one told me I could ask Jesus to come into my heart. I didn't trust my own father, and I didn't know how to trust a heavenly Father.

Mother took me to church, and I learned about the good man, Jesus, who was born in a manger, who did good deeds and said fine things; who was killed by bad men and then rose again and went back to heaven. Most of all we must remember to follow his example and live as he did. I tried. Oh, how I tried. I yearned to be good.

Early in the morning I would decide not to do anything bad that day. I would live as Jesus lived all day long. Yet somehow I always failed. Sometimes my goodness lasted no more than five minutes. One of my brothers would tease me or something else would cause me to think a bad thought or lose my temper. Then that day would already be ruined.

Our family had one "rock of faith" during all those years, my maternal grandmother. Although she died the night I graduated from high school, even yet I feel the power of her prayers for me. We held her in such high regard that whenever Mother had a bigger problem than usual, she wrote asking Grandmother to please pray for us.

My mother retired to overeating and reading voluminously to compensate for her unhappiness. On her yearly visits, Grandma's lectures on housekeeping did little good. She would rub the glass of the framed pictures to see if they had been washed since her visit last year, and usually they hadn't been. After Grandmother left, Mother always kept us learning the Bible verses Grandma had begun to teach us.

In her zeal to improve us, however, Grandmother forgot an important element: the joy of the Lord.

FOUR
Heartbreak

I made my debut at age twelve—that is, I made
my first entrance into social life. The two
girls next door, fifteen and seventeen years of age,
were already living in the great world of high
school. They told me they were having a party
and I remember thinking, "Oh, how wonderful!"

One summer day one of them said, "You
can come to our party if you want to." Want to?
With all my heart I was hoping I'd be invited.
I had exactly the right dress to wear.

My aunts had paid a dressmaker to make me a
pink organdy dress with layers of ruffles
on the short skirt. I was ready. I could scarcely
wait until the special night arrived. I floated
next door in a state of bliss, entering the great
world of belonging.

The talk buzzed around me about what went
on in high school and then the fellows and girls
decided to play games. The first suggestion

was "Spin the Bottle." One of the boys answered, "And have to kiss her?" He seemed to be looking at me, but I wasn't expecting to be kissed, so I thought he must mean someone else.

Instead they decided on "Wink 'Em." In this game a fellow stands behind a girl's chair and there's one empty chair. That boy winks at a girl and she tries to get away before the fellow behind her can hold onto her. The winking started, but no one even looked at me when his chair was vacant. At first I sat on the edge of my chair, expectantly. Then when I was ignored time after time, I tried to sink back into the upholstery.

At last the agony was over and the game was changed to Post Office. This time a boy watched the door and a girl came and asked for a stamp, letter, or package. Then both the girl and boy went inside the room and stayed a few minutes. They both came out shortly and a girl alternated keeping the door. I wasn't asked to come get any mail.

This game proved too slow for the guests, so next they played "Show." This time everyone who had a partner went into a darkened room and stayed.

Finally I was the only one left in the room. I went into the kitchen to help the hostess with the refreshments. I slunk out of the house as soon as I finished my fifth cup of punch and the accompanying sandwiches and cookies.

When I entered our house, there sat my mother reading. "How was the party?" she asked. One look at my face must have told her everything. I was a wallflower instead of a social butterfly. She came over and put her arm on my shoulder. That debacle made such a deep impression on me that I've never worn anything pink since.

That fall a new boy entered the eighth grade. His sister was a high school senior. I thought he was cute and said so to a friend. I was used to my brothers, but liking a boy was something else. The older sister came by my desk and left me a scathing note. "You keep your hands off my brother. When I want him to have a girl I'll choose her and it won't be YOU." Things were bearing down on me. This kind of emotional battering was as bad or worse than the physical battering had been.

Nothing has ever hurt me like the question I heard my mother ask my grandmother. It happened when the two of them were drinking tea in the living room of our home, and I, an ungainly, long-legged, awkward thirteen-year-old, had come into the kitchen. (No one knew there was a wave in my straight hair or that someday my string-bean frame, now usually bent over in a slouch, would fill out becomingly.) My mother was asking my grandmother, "Why should I have three hand-some boys and such a homely girl?"

I was instantly alert. "Who's she talking about?" I wondered, lifting a glass of water to take a sip.

Suddenly I froze in panic. "I'm the only girl she has—my mother's talking about ME!"

"It can't be true," I wanted to cry out as the

truth of her words sank into my consciousness. "It can't be true that my own mother thinks I'm homely." All the pain in the world seemed to hit me at once. Slowly and silently I poured the water back into the sink. I couldn't have forced down a drop. My throat was constricted. It couldn't hurt more. My world stood still. I suffered an agony of anguish. I felt totally rejected and unwanted. "My mother must be sorry I was ever born," I told myself.

As I tiptoed out, that thought felt like a whip that never stopped hitting me. There was no one to sympathize.

Grief is a heartbreaking burden at any time, but it's worst when it's borne alone, especially for a young person who has no perspective. Hearing my mother make that remark took away my last shred of dignity, my last dram of self-worth and confidence.

I remember saving my money to buy a bracelet, a wristwatch, and two rings, hoping people would look at the jewelry on my hands instead of at my face. For weeks I couldn't concentrate at school. I could think of little else, and every minute alone was an opportunity to brood about myself. I was a castaway.

In addition to that wound, I had another serious problem to face. I was asking myself: Where did I come from? Why am I here? Are people only the result of two biological forces coming together? Why are we sad so much? Why is this battle inside me between good and evil? Where are we going after death?

I was fumbling at the door of the entrance to the kingdom of God. I kept longing and searching for something, never realizing that what I needed was Someone.

Our minister often gave book reviews instead of sermons and he preached about doing good. In the back of our song book I kept looking for the word *hell* in the responsive readings. I was fascinated with that word. Finally at age fourteen, I was so troubled I went to this pastor and blurted out a cry for help. "If I die tonight," I told him, "I'll go to hell. What can I do?"

He answered, "Don't worry your pretty head— just go on being a good girl."

I was puzzled. I thought to myself, "Here he has gray hair and he doesn't know any more about life and death than I do." That day I mentally quit church even though my mother made me keep attending. My doubts, uncertainties, and perplexities were becoming disbelief. Finally one day I told her, "You can make me go now, but there'll come a day when I won't set foot inside a church." (That day came when I went away to college.)

We moved again and at age fifteen I entered my ninth school. There were forty-two students in our four-year high school at Ryderwood, Washington. It was a logging camp of about one thousand, twenty miles off the Seattle-Portland highway. Two hundred men lived in bunkhouses at the edge of town. The road in was through Cougar Flats, and sometimes we'd hear those animals' screams. We installed indoor plumbing to replace the watertap in the backyard and the little outhouse.

I hated that logging camp. It wasn't until I went back as an adult that I actually saw how beautiful Ryderwood is. Steep hills surrounded three sides. With so much rain in western Washington, it almost always was green. The trees had all been slashed with the first cutting, but within a year crimson fireweed and other plants made the slopes beautiful. In a short while maple and underbrush growth entirely covered the ugly scars of the logged-over land. Each fall the leaves turned rich colors: red, orange, yellow, and brownish hues.

The town itself consisted of one main street with a company store, a barber shop, a much needed and much used emergency hospital, a garage, a hotel with one wing reserved for schoolteachers, the pay office, and a theater with a dance hall upstairs. Houses lined the few other streets.

In this logging camp we had movies three evenings a week, with a dance on Saturday. When I decided not to go to the company church across town, my mother issued me one of her few ultimatums: "You get up and go to Sunday school or there's no going out on Saturday night!"

About two hundred people attended the Saturday night dances, which were well chaperoned. Even so, they were exciting because the girls would flirt and meet all the new fellows in town. I'd always rise and shine at

Mother's first call on Sunday morning. Friday and Saturday nights were too important to miss.

Sometimes on Fridays there were wrestling matches and prize fights, but I didn't like to go. My dad had quit beating me by then, and I wanted to forget all the violence I'd known as a child.

I was in the eleventh grade that year and inwardly I was saying, "Please—I'm here; like me, love me a little." I was working desperately hard at trying to make an impression. Hoping to be appreciated, I was coming on too fast. In school I was the one who answered every question first. I was so fearful I wouldn't be accepted I stuck out my neck at every opportunity so someone could chop it off or ignore me. I always ended up hurt. I was crushed whenever I learned there was a party to which my schoolmates hadn't invited me.

My eagerness to be accepted triggered one of the most dangerous moments of my life. Our town was excited when some workers caught a full-grown black bear. They built a strong cage for him over by the creek. A big packing box served as a shelter. Inside the fifteen-foot square of cement was a tree the bear could climb. An old oil drum served as an entrance to this area, with a heavy metal gate fastened outside across it. The top and sides of the cage were heavy wire mesh.

After school a number of us students walked over to see the big animal, but he refused to come out of his cage in spite of our pounding on the sides and top. Finally someone said,

"Let's go in and get him." All agreed, but no one wanted to go inside the enclosure. Finally the crowd turned on me, "Grizzly bear Ruth, ain't it the truth?" they chanted.

I was so scared I was trembling and I tried to hold back. Finally one girl said sarcastically, "You won't even do this one little thing for us?"

Hearing her jeering words, I cast aside all reason and judgment. I dropped onto my knees and started crawling through that oil drum entrance into the bear's cage. It took forever to get into the area, but then, as though pursued by demons, I raced around that tree and hurriedly pushed back through the opening. As I stood upright outside, the bear poked his nose out of his box and slowly ambled out into the enclosure where I'd been. The boys locked the cage behind me.

I turned to the crowd of students, expecting to be commended by the leader. Instead she spoke over her shoulder, "We couldn't be friends with such a stupid girl." Their hateful laughter echoed back as they walked away without me. I was playing the game of life to please the crowd and losing every inning.

I learned how lonely a person can feel in the midst of a crowd. I understand what it's like to feel rejected. I realize what it means to be a stranger in a strange land—that location being the Kingdom of the Accepted. It was a place I couldn't seem to enter. When these bad things are hurting us we think that nothing good can come from our distress. But those experiences were not a loss. It's possible now for me to greet strangers and talk with them anywhere and at any time. I know how they feel.

Soon after we arrived in Ryderwood I had one of the biggest surprises in my life. The high school guys wanted sex right away. I chose the older working men. They were serious.

Logging is a dangerous business. The loggers tried to grasp at some happiness before they might be killed. Once a rigger, one who climbs the high trees, was decapitated by a plunging wire. The workers placed his head and body behind a log while they finished the day's work. With trains running as far as twenty-five miles to bring out the logs, they didn't bother rerouting a special car when the man was already dead. Sometimes when a fellow was to quit or retire that day, he might be careless and get killed even his last hour on the job.

I'd gone to the show twice with an ordinary-looking, twenty-year-old "bucker," one who cut up the trees after they'd been cut down. He came into the house afterward and I made cocoa. As we were drinking it he said to me, "How would you like to make me some coffee every morning?"

"I don't drink coffee," I answered him.

"I'm not talking about cocoa or coffee," he said matter-of-factly. "You poor kid, you've been going to school all your life. We could get married if I take a day off next week."

"But I'm only fifteen and I haven't finished high school yet." As the slang was at that time, I was scared spitless.

"Nobody cares about school here. Last summer a girl of fifteen married my good friend and they're doing OK. Even ordered a new refrigerator from Sears this week. That makes their whole house filled with new furniture."

I looked at him in amazement. A woman, new furniture, plenty of food and drink were what mattered to some of the loggers.

One day Dad told me, "Don't be too good a girl or you won't have a good time." When I reported this to my mother, her face went white, she bit her lips, and her hands clasped tightly. She looked at me for a moment, then turned away. The next morning she sat down beside me at breakfast and asked, "How would you like to go to Longview High School for your senior year?"

Longview was the sawmill town on the Columbia River, about thirty miles away, where we shipped the logs to be cut into lumber. To me it was a big city with its eight thousand inhabitants. I clapped my hands and bounced up and down on my chair. I was overjoyed.

When we located a family who would provide breakfast and dinner and keep me from Sunday night to Friday each week, the lady of the house asked my mother, "Shall I tell Ruth what to do?"

Mother answered, "No, don't tell her—she knows what to do."

Years later I asked my mother how she could set a sixteen-year-old free in that town without any discipline. She said, "You never minded me. I didn't want that woman to try to make you mind—I knew she couldn't do it."

What a year that was. My mother's idea of clothes was what she had as a child: a dress. One was enough; she didn't care for any more.

Since I was leaving for the big town, we ordered a wool jersey dress from the catalogue. When it came, however, the narrow hem of the flared skirt rolled up in front and back. To make it even, I put buckshot in the hem. The heavy iron pellets would slide to one side when I sat down, or maybe to both sides, until the sag in one spot might be as much as two inches. Because the dress cost twenty-two dollars, I kept wearing it.

I made myself a new yellow smock with white collar and cuffs. I packed all my regular clothes, along with these two new ones, and left for school. Mother's last words to me were, "Don't wear the smock the first day."

I was alone. Alone. I felt as if the four walls were about to close in and crush me. I was frightened and insecure. I reacted by putting on a facade of bravery. I became brash, rude, and loud-mouthed. Almost my entire senior year was traumatic, although my mother made a supreme sacrifice when she sent me away. I had been not only her ears, but her social life as well. She'd have grieved if she'd known how things were going for me.

At the special tea they gave for incoming seniors at school, I was eager for refreshments. Often I'd spend all my lunch money for something on Monday and then I had to exist on two meals a day the rest of the week. At this senior welcoming party, I heaped my plate with tiny sandwiches and cookies—enough to make it look like the slabs of pie or hunks of cake we served in the logging camp. I couldn't understand why the others were snickering around me. I was a growing girl and I ate like a logger's daughter.

I went home from Saturday until Sunday afternoons, but I kept hearing school kids talk about a Sunday night church group. Mr. Tate, a high school teacher, went every week. Soon he started a Hi-Y Club for boys. I was amazed who attended his club because I knew what kind of lives those fellows lived.

I took Mr. Tate's English class the second semester and he was so nice he could be called meek. My dad always said, "Meekness is weakness," but Mr. Tate was meek in a strong sort of way. It was puzzling. When they called on him at the youth meeting, he never preached at us. He just lived his life loving people, good and bad. He loved God.

He surprised me by suggesting I go to his college. He gave me a little talking-to. He told me gently that the college would accept me because the high school faculty said I had ability even if I hadn't started studying yet. He hoped I'd apply myself.

That April my mother got sick and I quit school in the middle of the week. I returned to Ryderwood and enrolled there. In ten days my mother recovered. She had never asked about

46

my coming back home until a letter came from Mr. Tate with the words, "Hope your mother is better. I commend you to the friendship of the Man of Galilee. He has never failed me in like circumstances."

When Mother read my letter she looked at me in surprise. "Did you come home because I was sick?" she asked. "I thought you'd been expelled. Why, you pack your bags right now—you're going back to Longview High School this afternoon."

I did, and I'm a Christian today because of Mr. Tate.

FIVE
Student Days

One of the professors called Whitman College "The Wellesley of the West." Students in Washington state who couldn't get into Stanford University in California came to Whitman.

It was the most unlikely college in all the Northwest for a logger's daughter to attend. I was a misfit from the first moment. When I walked into pretentious Prentiss Hall carrying my shabby suitcase, I was overwhelmed. My tin trunk didn't help any, either. I felt I didn't belong there and since I'd already rejected myself, it was easy and only natural for the girls in the dorm to ignore and reject me.

The student across the hall from me had four fur coats. Many brought chairs and other furniture, as well as elaborate wardrobes. I had a new cotton Indian blanket to use as a bedspread. The remainder of my side of the room was bare except for the dresser, a desk, and lone chair.

The first evening I asked my roommate if she'd brought a white dress with her.

"Why?" she asked.

"Because you have to dress in white to be pledged to a sorority," I explained, "and we'll all be assigned to one."

How wrong could I be? At my suggestion she wrote her mother to mail hers. I had brought mine.

As days stretched to weeks, girls kept going to rush parties. Then, with the force of an overloaded locomotive bearing down on me, I admitted to myself the sober, solemn, and sickening truth: I was not being rushed and I would not be pledged. Others, too, began to be left out. Next to the time when my mother called me homely, this realization that I would never be a sorority girl hurt me more than anything else in my life. When I left college no one would call me a DG. That had been my dream.

As Christmas vacation neared, I'd had all I could stand. I was so hurt and deeply dissatisfied that I decided to quit school.

I started secretly taking my clothes down to the basement where I packed them, ready to take home with me. But you can't empty all your dresser drawers and your closet without someone knowing it. Margaret (who would later be killed while serving God in a far-off country) caught me in the hall when I returned from taking a load of clothing to my trunk. "Are you leaving school?" she asked. "Do you intend to be a quitter all your life?" Her voice was icy.

I was furious at her, but she had gotten through to me.

When Mother heard that one of the senior girls had told me, "Tell your folks to buy you some decent clothes," I returned to college with nine new outfits. Still, I had the same problems as before. I knew a wide gamut of profanity which I used profusely. I never tried to excuse my bad language; almost everyone in the logging camp swore.

During the last week of my freshman year there was a speaking contest for freshman girls. I entered and then left for home that evening before learning who had won. I rushed in to turn on the tub for a quick bath. I was packing, and, in trying to get everything together, I forgot the running water. It overflowed and soaked through onto the ceiling below. I knew I'd lost my ten-dollar room deposit since we were to get the money back only if we did no damage to the property. My guilt about the stained ceiling was all the worse because no one knew I'd done it.

Imagine my dismay a week later back in Ryderwood when I opened an envelope from the college as I walked home from the post office. Inside was a ten-dollar check, just that and nothing more. I was sure they'd found out about the ceiling. Now the authorities at Whitman were sending me my room deposit. They didn't want me back.

Here was the final rejection. All the years in logging camps, then Longview High School, now college. My heart was breaking. I didn't tell

my mother. Instead I pulled myself together
during dinner and talked more and louder than
ever.

Life had turned in another direction. Everything was changed by that ten-dollar check.
College wasn't for me, at least not Whitman. I
would never have set foot on that campus
again if I hadn't received another letter the next
day.

When I think of the times I've thought of
writing to someone and put it off, I thank God
that Kay didn't postpone writing to me when she
did. It was just a short note. She'd been a
contestant in the speaking contest too, only she
hadn't won. Now she congratulated me for
placing third and receiving the ten-dollar prize.
She hoped I'd enjoy spending the money.
Just that and nothing more, but it put the sun
back in the sky. The world of Whitman opened
up to me again after I thought it had closed.

In the fall of my sophomore year, I fell in love.
This young man was nearly perfect except
for one thing. He didn't go to church. I wanted
him to go so he'd make me go.

I wore his Phi Delt pin secretly. Finally one
night I told him I couldn't marry him because I
had no background and couldn't help him
as a community leader in his chosen work. I was
amazed and thrilled at his reaction. "I can't
live without you," he told me and begged
me to take his pin back again. I was ecstatic with
joy that he loved me so much. A few months
later when I was feeling depressed and unappre-

ciated, I gave him his pin again and he came hurrying to get me to take it once more. Being appreciated and cherished was to me like catnip is to a kitten. I gloried in it.

The third time I gave back his pin he calmly put it in his pocket. A short while later he gave it to someone who wasn't trying to play games with his heart the way I'd done. It was all over between us. It was the end of the world for me.

My heart broke partly for the wasted years when there might have been someone else, partly for my broken dreams, but most of all because I'd been such a fool not to appreciate what I had. For me there was a tomorrow, however, because fine as this young man was, and in spite of how much I loved him, he wasn't the one for me.

After my junior year I was visiting at home for a few days when my father asked me to go with him to see his latest lady friend. Although I was disgusted at him, I agreed. I made myself as unattractive as I could. I tousled my hair, wore my oldest dress, and put on bobby socks with high heels. No doubt Dad had bragged about me to her and I was fighting with the only weapon I had, myself. I went home as pleased as could be for what I'd done, but I didn't know she'd get the last laugh on me.

Near the end of August, this woman threatened to tell her hot-tempered husband about this affair, and in the ensuing arguments, Dad bought her a new car with the money designated for my senior year's expenses. I couldn't afford to go back.

I spent the winter selling shoes while living with my two aunts. They went off to work. They came home at night to a cold house. They cooked a meal. The next day was the same. I helped as much as I could. Although my aunts' lives seemed dull, and their future looked bleak, I had to admit something. In spite of their circumstances, they had an inner happiness that the doldrums of their workaday world couldn't explain. God was real to them, although they couldn't express it to others.

One Sunday on our walk to church we passed a new young man. He said hello to us and then after we arrived at the service, he entered also. He sang all the hymns and at the close of the benediction he hurried over and asked us to ride home in his car. As he let us out, he asked me for a date. I suggested we go double, and we went in a group several times. Then he asked me to go to dinner with him. He was a debonair car salesman, fifteen years older than I was.

At that time my life consisted of parties, picnics, good times. I had no idea that tragedy was near.

SIX
Nightmare

My life was shattered into a million pieces
that June night when I was twenty-one years old.
I lived an eternity in a single minute.

My date, the car salesman, and I were laughing
together as we drove the thirty miles into
Seattle for dinner. In the city I had such a
premonition of disaster that I phoned my aunt
long distance to ask if I could stay overnight
with my cousin. Knowing I had to go to work
the next morning at the store, she told me to
come back home.

The tires on his car were thin and as we rode
along we skidded where water had collected
in a low place from recent rains. I didn't scream
as the car shot out of control—there wasn't
time. As I sucked in my breath to brace myself,
another auto loomed from around the curve.

SMASH—our car crashed head-on into the
other auto with a shuddering sound of rending

steel and splintered glass, then ricocheted and careened wildly from curb to curb. My date hung onto the steering wheel with all his might, and by leaning from side to side, we finally stopped.

For one dreadful second I felt unbelievably intense pain. Then instantly there was no more suffering.

Looking out the car window we discovered we were resting within inches of a steep bank. Directly below the seventy-foot cliff were the murky, choppy, hungry billows of Lake Washington.

Even though I'd missed being drowned, I'd gone where no one wants to go—through the windshield. There in the glass, a circle was cut out as smoothly as if my head had been a glass-cutter.

Other cars stopped. I felt I couldn't move, but kind hands helped me out of the car. I had the strange sensation that wet rain was coursing down my face. I glanced downward and saw that blood was streaming onto the front of my dress in a six-inch swath, clear to the hemline, and plopping onto the parking strip. Gentle hands laid me flat on the pavement. An onlooker handed me a snow-white handkerchief to try to stop the bleeding. Then more hankies came. An ambulance with sirens screaming delivered me to a hospital emergency room.

One good thing came out of that dreadful accident. It took away my fear of riding in an automobile. I knew if you're hurt badly enough, you don't feel it. That's how it was with me—I felt absolutely no pain while the young intern took twenty-seven stitches to patch up my face. Both he and the nurse kept asking if I wanted an anesthetic, but I was in shock. For more than an hour I lay on the operating table.

During my stay the entire hospital staff showed a tenderness and kindness I didn't understand until I saw my face later. Then I could comprehend the compassion that even professional medics couldn't help expressing. I was that badly scarred.

Those days are an unbelievable nightmare in my life. My aunts kept on working (our family policy was that we didn't visit anyone sick in the hospital). No one notified my mother. Through it all I was desperately alone. No one prayed with me or mentioned that God had spared my life and especially my eyes. I was in a pit of sorrow.

When I went back to my aunts' home, my black eyes had faded to a bilious yellow. The scars on my face stood out like streaks of crimson lipstick. When my aunt glanced at me, she turned white, then swayed dizzily. Reaching up, she clutched the mantel to keep from fainting.

That moment I wished with all my heart that the car had plunged off the cliff and I had drowned. But worse was to come. The first time I found the courage to walk outside the house, I met a neighbor I'd baby-sat for years before. This friend took one look at me and gasped, "Oh, what awful scars!" All through the years before the accident I believed I was homely. Now it was worse. I felt I was ghastly.

Two results came from that heartbreaking summer. One was such a tremendous relief that I felt as if I had quit dragging a dead horse along behind me.

One of my aunt's favorite topics of conversation was my dad. "He's a cad, a disappointment," she used to say. "There never was such a poor excuse for a father as yours." She didn't need to tell me, I already knew it. Then she'd continue her recital of his sins and shortcomings. "You've got to amount to something to make up for your father," she'd say.

When she talked like that I felt I had to carry the load of my dad's sins piled on top of my own personal regrets and torments. It was almost too much for one human to endure, but my aunt kept it up.

Finally one day when she'd been especially caustic in her criticism, censure, and prodding, I'd had all I could stand. I answered, "How can you expect me to amount to anything with such a father?"

I thought the world of her and we had a beautiful relationship, but she looked as if I'd slapped her. Her mouth fell open and her eyes filled with tears. She turned and hurried out of the room. After that she never said an unkind word about my dad again.

When she quit criticizing him to me, she cut loose a binding shackle in my life. She freed me from a past I did not cause and could not alter.

A second result of that accident was my realization that I'd need more education, since I was facing life scarred. (I didn't know then that in five years the cruel marks would fade, and that in ten years they'd be even less noticeable.) When you're twenty-one, today is what matters; and I knew I must get my college degree. I was dead earnest and intended to study hard. By then my inner scars were hurting worse than those on the outside. I also believed that everything would turn to ashes, no matter what I did, but I wanted to prove I could graduate.

I started my senior year low in spirit. Then, "Papa" Pratt, my voice teacher, gave me the encouragement I needed. At my first voice lesson he asked how my summer was.

"Look at my face and you'll see my life is ruined," I answered sadly.

"What do you mean?" he asked.

"These scars are from an auto accident . . ." I pointed to my face.

He left the piano, came near, and squinted at me closely. "I don't see any scars," he said calmly.

From the goodness of his heart he did more for me than anyone else could have done. I sang in his college choir, traveled with his glee club, and had leads in *Hansel and Gretel* and *Pirates of Penzance*. For the first time the conservatory gave an Honorable Mention. Papa Pratt was doing all he could to build my self-confidence and self-esteem. Still, I didn't accept his invitation to visit his church. God can't do anything for us when we shut him out of our lives as I was doing.

Papa talked one of his voice students, a young assistant professor, into dating me. This prof was a big puzzle in my life because his father was a preacher, but Art wanted no part of God. I couldn't think of anything finer than to have your dad love you and love God, too. We fought about faith on our dates until I was glad when Christmas vacation came so I could go back to see the man I'd left behind, the car salesman.

I was like a ship on the sea of life, whose anchor, compass, and pilot wheel had been thrown overboard. I felt as if I was racing down a freeway on which the traffic signals and road signs had been removed; as if I were flying in a pilotless plane toward an airport without landing lights.

SEVEN
"There Is No Hope!"

Just as nature deplores a vacuum, so does the human heart. Everyone needs to believe in something. No one tried harder than I did my senior year of college. I wanted to believe in myself and forget my past and be happy doing it, but it was useless to try. I was moody and often depressed. I ended up keeping busier and feeling more wretched. I was in an agonizing struggle for certainty.

Then a new idea came on the scene, so mind-changing it caused another turnaround in my thinking. In my senior year of high school my preconceived ideas of manhood had been reversed when I met Mr. Tate and learned that meekness is not necessarily weakness. I'd been battered by a physically strong man who could beat me because he had the brawn to do it. From Mr. Tate I'd learned that strength of character and faith do not depend on brute physical force.

What I heard from my professor in an advanced English course was stark, raw, and shocking. "There is no God," he said. This man was a confirmed atheist who spent as much time expounding this theory as he did teaching us literature. He was so charming with his dark hair, brown flashing eyes, and superior intelligence that I was captivated. "God is dead if he ever . . ." was an expression he often repeated. His ringing laughter would punctuate his comments about "inane people who need a crutch of religion when they're not even cripples." He seemed to have life all wrapped up in a package with no loose corners or dangling strings. He seemed to direct all his charm and persuasion on those of us who had any background of faith.

Until I met this professor, I always thought it was only the fool who said there was no God. When he started his campaign to tell us why he'd come to an atheistic point of view he gave the usual objections. So much suffering in the world. Children malformed, hurt, and neglected. War. Why doesn't God stop people from killing each other? His logic was sparkling. Then he stopped his arguments and took a long look at the class. "Is there anyone here who believes in God?" he asked. The question was a challenge. Several hands went up, including mine.

The next week he began his talk with the words, "I beseech you, brethren and sisters, to give up your religious Dos and Don'ts." His words made me uncomfortable, but the class roared with laughter. "Give up such ideas," he implored, "and believe there is no God. There's nothing to worry about because you can do anything you please, whenever you want—this is complete freedom."

I wanted this professor to like me, but even more I longed for what he promised: complete freedom. Still, he hadn't yet convinced me there was no God.

"Did God send that flood to destroy that home yesterday?" he asked, knowing some of us had seen a house fall into swollen Mill Creek. When lovely Peggy, a campus favorite, died of pneumonia, he queried, "Where was God when she was so sick yesterday?"

By the end of the semester, while I was still searching for an answer to life, I tried to believe that atheism was true. If there was no God hiding up somewhere with a big stick to use on me, then I wouldn't be clobbered as an adult as I'd been in my childhood. I even called myself an atheist, but I was flooded with doubts about it all. I couldn't get away from one especially persistent and nagging idea, that sometime after death I might have to answer for what I'd done on earth.

During this time of trying to decide about the existence of God, I learned a valuable lesson. I learned I could doubt my doubts.

The last assignment I handed in to this professor I titled "There Is No Hope." Before he began to read my paper aloud to the class he told us, "This is by one who faces reality unafraid." I wanted to scream at him, "I'm afraid all the time. I'm scared because of what I remember from yesterdays; I'm frightened for all the tomorrows and pained for what might happen today." Here is an excerpt from that article:

Standing on the brink of entering the great arena of Life, I have one sincere conclusion to guide me—there is no hope of ever further enjoying anything. If I should reach that long dream of something I want to attain, it will turn into ashes and there'll be nothing left.

So why not end it all? Why do I keep striving, yearning and hoping with a petulance born of despair when I'm confident there's nothing ahead?

When we come to the end of life, we find our muscles are cramped and tired and we're past true enjoyment. It's night and the lights have all gone out in the world.

There is no hope!

But all the while there's a small nudging inside me that says, "Maybe the knowledge and philosophy of atheism is wrong. Maybe there is a Supreme Being after all? Could the teaching which the prof says is ignorance be the truth and the light? Factors that could make me free?"

When he finished reading my paper, he commented, "Excellent paper, but you're free now if you want to be." He gave me an *A*.

Oh, how I wanted to be free from the memories

of my childhood. From the fears of this present day with all the iniquity in my own heart, the jealousy, envy, gossip, and hatred. From the dread of tomorrow. I'd learned the hopelessness of hoping and the futility of everything. I had little reason to live any longer.

Something was missing. I didn't know what was needed to make me a whole person. I had no idea how to straighten out my life.

EIGHT
On the Edge

If any of the Sigma Chi fraternity singers
serenading our girls' dormitory my last Saturday
night at Whitman College had looked up at
me, he'd never have guessed the turmoil I was
suffering. Instead he'd have seen a blonde,
twenty-two-year-old girl of medium height
curled up on the window ledge, her hands
wrapped around her knees. With my naturally
wavy, honey-colored hair shining in the
moonlight, the beams did not reveal the strange
scars on my face that crossed my nose and
forehead, scars still visible from the auto
accident. No one had suggested I have plastic
surgery on my face.

Least of all would anyone imagine that I was
teetering there trying to decide whether to roll
myself over the ledge of the roof's parapet
and plunge to my death on the pavement below.
No one would ever be sure whether or not
I did it deliberately. My agony on earth would
end.

As I peered down from three stories up, it looked like a long way to the ground.

This was not a premeditated plan. It was a spontaneous impulse.

The soft sounds of the singing tore at my heart and added to my unhappiness. I don't recall if this serenade was an engagement announcement or the last farewell to us graduating in two days. It might as well have been the end of the world because it was the end of mine. Commencement was not a beginning in my life. I felt like the Indian on the horse in the picture called "End of the Trail." I had had it! Life was too much. I had lost the battle. I was absolutely at the bottom and I was desperate. I hadn't found the answers to my life's problems.

At college I had lived only for myself and what I could get. I had been as greedy for honors as a thirsty, dying sufferer out on the desert, trying to get water to drink. I had tried for every possible office and recognition and had had a measure of success.

I was longing with all my heart for the finer things of life. Prentiss Hall, where I lived, was decorated with elegant art objects and deep, luxurious oriental rugs. But my logging camp home was waiting for me when I graduated and finished summer school. No teaching position was available.

I had a gleaming new diamond ring stashed away in my dresser drawer. I had been both amazed and dismayed that past week when I received an insured box containing a lovely engagement ring glistening on the purple velvet lining. My car salesman friend had mailed it to me. I didn't love him, but I was starving for someone's love.

Everything seemed wrong as I faced what appeared to be a big black abyss ahead. Everywhere was uncertainty. Something vital and crucial was missing.

My despair was beyond any tangible success. Except for a job opening, my physical needs had been met. No new outfit would satisfy. No tour would bring satisfaction. The pleasures of the moment were not enough. My troubles were deeper than anything visible.

What I needed was a reason to keep on living. I was in a state of spiritual bankruptcy and self-repudiation. I had rejected myself. I sat on that window ledge, longing for a meaning to life, while I had death within the twitch of my muscles.

I was always searching for something, but my searching had been in vain. In spite of all the students and teachers around me, I lived in frightening loneliness. I believed that moment that nothing could possibly make things worse for me. Life was piteous and I felt a sense of impending doom.

Students, teachers, and others at that college in southeastern Washington state would have been surprised to learn that a successful senior could be in such anguish. They had no idea of how I hugged every hurt to my heart. The wounds of childhood as well as those of my teen and adult years were never far from me. My freshman year at this school had

been catastrophic, learning the social amenities
I'd missed acquiring during my growing-up
years. My sophomore year I'd fallen in love while
at the same time getting on probation for
not studying. My junior year was marked by the
broken love affair. My senior year I'd learned to
study, but it was all futile because I felt battered
inside.

I was still hungering for approval and
acceptance. Along with this was a heavy sense of
guilt, because I would not forgive anyone.
I grasped every opportunity to recall and recount
the worst of what had happened to me.

That night, sitting on the windowsill
contemplating suicide, I swayed a little bit with
the excitement of it all. Everyone would
talk about it and would try to remember a last
contact with me. Maybe they'd think they
should have done more—Ah, that's what I
wanted: for them to be sorry and bewildered and
shocked and wish they'd paid more attention
and been nicer to me. My egotism made me want
them to go through some of the same regrets I
experienced every day. I gloated at the prospect.

This was a critical moment.

For a second I rocked gently back and forth like
a clock pendulum. The Sigma Chis began
their last song about a girl of their dreams being
the only girl "of all the girls I know." Well,
they weren't talking about me because I was
the dream only of a man fifteen years older than
I, a man I didn't love. I stopped swinging
and listened intently. The next phrase of the song
mentioned an angel.

"Angel?" That would mean heaven and I knew the old song was right: "Everybody talkin' 'bout heaven, ain't goin' there." I wasn't going there because if what they said about God being holy was true, then he couldn't stand me. There was too much badness in my life, known and unknown to others. Heaven was beyond the realm of possibilities.

"To be or not to be, that is the question..." To die or not to die. That was my problem. Suddenly the next phrase of the song caught and held me like an invisible pair of arms encircled around my shoulders. It was as if someone who loved me had enfolded me in a gossamer, eiderdown shawl. What gave me this joy was that the singers were describing me, "When the moonlight beams on the girl..."

In that instant, from my high perch on the third-floor windowsill, I made a split-second decision. I thought, if I hurtle down to the pavement, I'll be a broken, crushed corpse. I won't be a girl with the moon beaming on me anymore. Divine Power outside me used that sweet love song to keep me from killing myself. All at once I decided to live.

As the singers turned to go back to their fraternity house, I untangled myself from my position and fell across my bed. I cried far into the night. I was thankful the dorm was empty so I could weep my heart out all alone.

I sobbed uncontrollably for all the wasted years. For all the opportunities I missed to do something for someone else besides myself. For being so self-centered. For times when I did

wrong willfully although I knew what was right. For saying so many cutting, catty, sarcastic remarks about people and, worse yet, for saying so many hurtful, harmful things *to* them.
I wept for pretending to be a success when I was a phony and a hypocrite.

During my four years at college I'd learned how enormous are the riches and the breadth, width, depth, and height of learning—and how little I knew. I'd been amazed to discover that all the people on earth could be piled into the Grand Canyon. From a study of astronomy I realized how vast the universe is and how small a whisper we know of it.

At twenty-two years of age I saw life as an endurance contest between what *was* in the eternal and my secret longing that the situations around me could somehow be different. I didn't realize that I was the one who needed changing, who needed to start life anew.

I hadn't the slightest inkling of what would take place within twenty-four hours. The very next day links of circumstance would start fastening together. My viewpoint and attitude would change. In another atmosphere, I'd adopt other customs and emphases. Within five months my motivations and actions would alter. Another world was waiting for me, where by my own choice I'd enter the kingdom of God.

I was about to discover the eternal Source in whom I could be abundantly satisfied for the rest of my life; soon even my battered past would be adequately dealt with.

NINE
Road
to Peace

After the Sigma Chi serenade, did I wake up the next morning feeling cheerful, relieved, and grateful to be alive? It wasn't that way. As my eyes opened, I thought, "Another day, maybe worse." Self-pity was consuming me.

Part of the problem was that my mother was arriving. My college graduation was the culmination of all her dreams for me. She had sacrificed a lot to pay my expenses, but from her point of view to see me graduate would make it all up. During my growing-up years she had talked about my becoming a college graduate as if I would then enter a new and ultimate world of attainment. To myself I was saying "So what?"

Gloom surrounded me like a heavy curtain that made everything look dark. At breakfast, my favorite pecan rolls tasted better because

I knew I was eating them on my last Sunday in this dining room. The orange juice was richer. The eggs with tiny slivers of crisp bacon had a new taste to me, as I knew that this was my next to last breakfast on this campus. I savored every bite.

By the time I finished the last cup of coffee, I was eager to hear the preacher from Seattle who'd speak at the eleven o'clock baccalaureate service. I had been to church only a few times during my four years at this school. Surely this last message would be for me.

A little after ten the seniors lined up ready to march in. Once seated, I waited expectantly to hear the sermon. I needed words of reassurance, an answer to life's problems. This speaker was my last shred of hope. "The creeds of Christendom," he began, "are a priceless heritage marking as they do the long road mankind has trod in its search after God."

I knew all about the long road I had trod, but my treading hadn't been any search after God. I'd hunted for everything else: pleasure, popularity, prominence, prosperity. I didn't know what he was talking about when he mentioned "the unsurpassed wisdom of the teachings of Jesus."

I wanted to interrupt him and ask, "What's that got to do with me? Jesus has gone back to heaven."

The talk ended with the statement, "To rediscover a reasoned basis for a living faith in God means a long, hard road stretching before you as long as life shall last."

Hearing those words made me furious! I was angry at him for using the word "adventure" and then saying "long, hard road." I wanted to stand up in that service and yell at him, "Life is *not* an adventure! It's what you said: a *long* road that turns into a long, *hard* road!" I was disgusted at him for pretending to know anything about God when he talked like that.

I remembered some words I'd heard long ago that described my state of mind, not realizing they came from the Bible: "... oppressed ... afflicted ... like a lamb before its shearers is dumb, so he opened not his mouth" (Isaiah 53:7). I felt oppressed and afflicted. This had been my last chance at finding a reason for living.

The moment we rose to file out was the lowest moment of my adult life. I accepted what was to be for what already was. What *is* will be in spite of our willing and wishing it otherwise. I believed that nothing could ever change. I faced the truth that whenever a crisis comes there are two ways to meet it. First, a person can run away, as I'd almost done the night before, and thus end it all. Or there's the second and even harder way of not dodging it, but facing the consequences. I could do nothing but accept my misery, and that was what I had to do. Keeping on was the most difficult future I could face.

Because our college was named to honor Marcus Whitman, the martyred missionary, it made some token gestures toward being a Christian school. As entering freshmen and again as graduating seniors, we made a pilgrimage to his grave. (It also had compulsory chapel—although in all the talks and programs, I never heard that God loved me and had a plan for my life. No one ever said that Jesus Christ wanted to be my Savior and the Lord of my life, or that I could have a relationship with him.)

That Sunday afternoon in the brief ceremony at the Whitman monument I heard once again the account of how the pioneer doctor visited this location in 1835 and saw the Indians' great need for medical attention. A year later he returned with his bride, Narcissa, to found the mission.

How fulfilling, I thought, for them to give their lives in such a great cause. Next the gallant physician rode horseback alone across the continent to get help for his mission. He urged Congress to take more interest in what was then the Oregon Territory. Because of this heroic and perilous journey, many believe he saved this great wealth of land for the United States.

Again I was grieved at hearing the story of the tragic drowning of the Whitmans' tiny daughter; and then, following a measles epidemic, the massacre of all fourteen persons at the mission by the Cayuse Indians.

My reverie and sense of respect for the Whitman party gave way to the present when the last bugle sounded.

Someone in the crowd asked, "Anyone need a ride?"

Like the singing of the Sigma Chi love song, this was for me another moment of destiny.

"Yes," I answered, not noting who had spoken. Many people standing there might have asked us to ride. It turned out to be the pastor of a church in Walla Walla. When you ride twenty-five miles with a person, you have time to get acquainted, and we did. Once I'd gone to his church when he showed some pictures of Europe.

As we traveled I kept wishing we'd never get back to the dorm. I knew who would be awaiting me there, and I dreaded the encounter.

Occasionally during the year the salesman who'd sent me the diamond ring drove the three hundred miles across the state of Washington to visit me. Girls in the dorm helped me eat the chocolates he brought and I was proud of the beautiful roses he sent. I enjoyed going to nice eating places with him. Now I didn't want to hurt him, but he wasn't the haven for my heart. But there he was, and I had to level with him.

I suggested we drive out the same road I'd just traveled. The wheat fields would be a remote place for us to talk.

As soon as the car stopped, I pulled out the ring. Holding it in my hand but still looking ahead, I told him as gently as possible how much I appreciated his friendship and kindness. I hadn't expected this ring, however, and I wanted him to take it back.

He sucked in a short breath, then expelled the air violently. A chill of uneasiness spread over me. Then his jaw clenched tightly and his eyes appeared to be glazed. A red flush of hatred quickly spread over his face and neck.

When his eyes met mine I'd never seen such anger, even in my father's face. Totally enraged, he spat out the words, "You're going to get a rich settlement from your car accident."

"Oh, no," I explained. "I already settled for double the medical expenses."

On hearing this he raised slightly on his seat and seemed ready to jump some place. His fists clenched so tightly his knuckles showed white. His fingers spread like claws with a motion as if he wanted to crush something between his palms. He kept repeating this movement and I sensed that what he wanted to strangle was my neck. "You idiot, you fool . . ." his words hissed at me.

I was terrified. Here I was on this lonely, little-traveled road, miles from any dwelling. I knew I had to use my wits if I were to get out of this alive. All at once, I knew how much I wanted to live.

I tried to soothe him. "I'm sure we can work this out," I cajoled him, knowing that all I really wanted was to get myself safely out of his car and back to school. Finally he calmed down and drove me to the dorm. With each passing mile I was longing more and more to wear that cap and gown and march across the platform to receive my sheepskin. I realized how much I valued my future even if it was unknown.

Far into that night I thought about this sequence of events. The past two days seemed parallel. I wondered if I hadn't been as close to death this Sunday afternoon, in his car on that lonely road, as I'd been the night before on the window ledge. On Saturday it was death by my own hands; on Sunday, death by his. The thought was staggering.

Along with the satisfaction of being alive and whole, I also felt an uncanny nostalgia every time I remembered those martyred missionaries. They'd lived for something and died for something. They had more than I had—they had purpose. I envied them.

The first faint rays of morning light were breaking over the eastern mountain's rim when I finally fell asleep. I awoke refreshed even with so little rest; I was actually tingling.

What was it? What excited me so?
A dream? No, nothing I could remember.
A vision? No, I felt too learned for that.
Some idea? Yes, that's it.

Evidently I'd mulled it over in my sleep all night.

It had to do with our graduating class. One of the senior fellows was going to be a Christian minister—why not two of us working for God? Couldn't I be a missionary? I could teach in a mission school in a foreign country. That way I'd travel as well as be sure of a job. I'd heard they appealed for missionary volunteers at a tent meeting over on the edge of town, but of course I wasn't there to hear it myself.

It was a new thought for me: working for God. The Almighty would be lucky to have me, since so few were answering what was called missionary service. All morning while packing my clothes and belongings I got excited. Then, with a shock of reality, I thought, how could I work for God when I'd turned my back on him? I didn't even belong to a church. I wasn't going anywhere but back to my logging camp.

All during the graduation exercises I tried to be practical. I kept debating back and forth. Really, now, God did need some reinforcements even if I didn't know him well enough to ask him for a job. I remembered Mr. Tate, my high school teacher, who'd gone to some special school in California before he went to Thailand to be president of a college. I knew nothing about it except that the name of the town was San Anselmo.

I didn't realize that all God wants is a ready, willing heart and he'll do the rest. When you take one step toward him, he's there like a concerned, anxious, loving parent who watches over a toddler. When you fall, God will catch you and help you start over again. During commencement somehow I knew I'd been dead wrong in thinking there was no hope. I was aware there was something to live for, after all, even though it was intangible and too far off to be real.

One of the speakers on the platform that day said something I never forgot. "Anyone can make a splash," he told us, "but you be like the strong tide." I'd tried, oh, how I'd tried all my life to make a splash, but I hadn't succeeded. Maybe I should try to be like the strong tide. But I didn't know how to start and I didn't have the willpower either.

The culmination of our four years of college was a banquet at the Marcus Whitman Hotel. During the meal, Tom, another graduate and a professor's son, was across the table from me.

"Now that you've graduated, Ruth," he said to me, "what are you going to do?"

"I don't know," I told him. "I go to Seattle tomorrow to attend the university summer school, but I don't have any plans after that."

"You don't sound very happy about it all," he remarked.

"I'm not," I told him. "There's a school in California I'd like to attend, but I don't know anything about it."

"What's the name?" he asked.

"San Anselmo."

"San Anselmo?" He leaned forward with a big smile. "Why, my bride and I are going there in September. Why don't you go too? My father will recommend you. What's your church?"

"I don't belong to a church, but I met a minister yesterday coming back from the Whitman monument."

"Great." Tom's smile was even broader. "There's a trustee here tonight from Spokane— I'll introduce you."

A coincidence? Destiny? God's plan for my life?

Six hundred people at that dinner, and I sat

opposite the one person who could help me get accepted at that school. Only God could manage that.

So, instead of attending the university that summer, I went to San Anselmo in September. All the while I had two secrets. The first was that I knew there was hope in the world if only I could find it. The second was more disturbing: I knew there was a vast river of troubled water between God and me. I didn't know any bridge over this great gulf that separated me from him. It was all wrapped up in the mystery of a reason for living and my fear of dying. I didn't have anything to believe in but myself, yet sometimes I hated myself. I hadn't started moving yet and nothing in my life had changed. But now I believed there was such a thing as peace for a troubled, restless spirit like mine.

TEN
Circle of Prayer

The San Francisco Theological Seminary was
a school for the training of ministers,
missionaries, and church workers. Today they
probably wouldn't admit someone like me,
but they accepted me then.

At seminary, the single men lived in a large
dormitory while the single women stayed
in a big old house with a housemother. What
remarkable individuals these young women
were! Every evening after dinner we'd sit quietly
while one read from the Bible. Then there'd
be a circle of prayer. They sounded as if they'd
turned their whole lives over to God. I'd
never heard anything like this before. I tried to
miss this praying, but I couldn't because
everyone expected me to attend.

It was the way these girls prayed that baffled
me most. If someone was going somewhere,
they'd ask Jesus to be with her as if he was still

earth. They'd pray for God
study for an exam and even ask his
their best in answering the questions.
it they were presumptuous to bother
with such trivialities when he was busy
ning the universe. Yet all seemed to want
what God wanted more than their own desires.
They called themselves God's children.

I was unyielding. I wasn't ready to hand myself
over to anybody or to any cause. I wasn't
sure about anything connected with faith. I
knew I wasn't God's child. My heart was
congealed hard and I didn't permit it to thaw.

All unknown to me, though, their praying
was slowly melting the ice around my heart,
slowly chipping away the layers of stone in my
consciousness. But no one mentioned my
giving my heart to Jesus or opening the door to
him so he could come in and cleanse me
and live his life through me. Deep down, though,
I knew I was different from these others even
if by now no one could tell I was from a logging
camp. I'd learned to tone down my loud-
mouthed, arrogant bragging and boasting which
I'd used to shield my inadequacies. I was
learning to control my swearing. My tremendous
drive for success was beginning to give way
to a new realization, the gentlest whisper, the
strange inner feeling that these girls had
something more important than any of my
distant goals of accomplishment and travel.

One girl in the dorm, named Jan, bothered me
most. Her looks left much to be desired and
her clothes were pathetic. She had no money to

buy the little extras the rest of us did. She had to study harder and work longer on her assignments, but she kept thanking God for peace and joy. Peace and joy? Finally when we were alone for a minute I asked her how she could have peace and joy with all the grief in the world.

She smiled sweetly and answered, "That's why Christ died."

Her words made the fog of my thinking even deeper and darker. But in spite of Jan's disappointing answer, I started reading the New Testament, chapter after chapter, and the eyes of my understanding began to open.

I was like a small child in a candy factory, and the printed pages became sweeter all the time—clearer and more alive. As a result of this reading I became even more conscious of my sins, but most of all I didn't want any of the students and especially the faculty to know I wasn't a Christian. I was too proud to ask for help. I was afraid if they found out the truth they'd say I didn't belong at seminary and send me home.

Being there and not being a Christian was like trying to learn to swim while lying on a piano bench—without getting into the water. I had a steady, haunting impression I'd given my life and ability for God's work, but I hadn't given myself to him.

Sin did not march before my eyes. It was a constant, unbearable companion. The ambivalence of my life seemed more than I could endure. I felt like the world's biggest hypocrite. I'd been ignoring God all these years. I'd refused to learn or follow his leading and guidance. I'd been stiff-necked and rebellious. Now, of all the impossible things to happen to me, I was trapped with all these true Christians. It was my version of hell.

Although I kept going through the motions, my soul was in agony. My spirit was groaning with grief. The experiences of everyday life at the seminary were getting intolerable.

Finally, the night before my twenty-third birthday, I knelt beside my bed. I was silently pleading for help. I was longing, waiting, and crying. I didn't know what to pray or how to begin. I'd always bartered with God, telling him I'd try to do better or do some specific thing if he'd grant me my request. I had a fear of God and what he might do to me, but that night I wanted to get near to him. I prayed differently. I needed him so desperately. I told him what was in my heart: my hatred of my father, how unfair he was, the hurts and heartaches I'd endured. I poured out everything to him in a way I'd never done before.

I was finally broken. I couldn't bear to live with my past another moment. All the disappointments and discouragements, all that I'd done and what had been done to me, I confessed to God. A giant wave of conviction, contrition, and repentance flooded me.

Then—my burden was lifted! God touched my hurting, willful heart, my intellect, and emotions. My world was changed.

That moment was deeper than thought or

feeling or knowledge or will, but it was all of them and more. No lights flashed, no bells rang, but it was as real as if sight and sound had combined. The message was more distinct than anything on earth. I was conscious of the words, "As far as the east is from the west, so far has he removed our transgressions from us" (Psalm 103:12).

I didn't have to give up my sins. God took them away into the sea of his forgetfulness. He threw them into the wastebasket of life. I knew I was renewed and cleansed inside.

I felt exhilarated. Peace filled my being. A cloak of divine security, a sense of protectiveness enveloped me. It was as if an infinite ocean of love was pouring over me, surrounding me, guarding me, and comforting me.

At that sacred moment, I knew the meaning of the word *rapture*. I was conscious that the words were true in my life: "For God so loved the world that he gave his only begotten Son that I who believe in him shall not perish but now have eternal life" (John 3:16, paraphrased).

God loved me, and I believed it. It was my "leap of faith." I believed in him and loved him, so now I had eternal life. It was the birthday of my new life in Christ. I was born again.

I knew I was washed clean and changed. I had a quiet, yet awesome assurance that God accepted me. It was more than a feeling—it was a relationship with a Person. I was now a part of God's "Forever Family." Other Christians were my brothers and sisters.

If God accepted me, then I could accept myself.

This realization opened up a new dimension of thinking and living.

I was under New Management. I'd found the secret for happiness: trust in Jesus. Now my motivation, priorities, and goals were Christ-centered.

At last I'd found the love and acceptance I'd longed for my whole life through. All the abuse, battering, and rejection were pushed aside when God took me just as I was. The divine approval I felt gave me a greater sense of satisfaction than I'd ever dreamed possible. For the first time I felt free.

I knew Jesus Christ had died for me. He had taken my sins away when he bore my guilt along with the sins of the world on the cross. His shed blood had washed me clean. With the magnitude of this truth came the desire to return God's love in worship and thanksgiving.

I could scarcely believe I could change so much. True, I went about doing the same things as the day before: classes and study and dormitory life. But what a difference. Now there was a purpose to everything. I had a security of inner resources because the power of God had been released in my life.

ELEVEN
Victory

Just as an adopted child brings along a repertoire of personal characteristics, good and bad, I brought mine into the family of God. I still had my weaknesses, shortcomings, problems, complexes, fears, memories, habits, foibles, and hangups. I was a beginner in the Christian walk, and I stumbled and limped along as best I could.

I knew that Jesus was alive in my heart and I'd never walk alone again. But the more the light of Christ was shed on my life, the more my imperfections showed and had to be dealt with. As I read the Bible and prayed, I realized that certain practices in my life had to be weeded out.

Even with the power of divine help, it was difficult and often still is. Sometimes I've felt like a little girl trying to walk on the edge of a thawing winter wheat field. In the eastern part of Washington state, sometimes the ground freezes to several feet deep. Then a freak thaw may melt the earth down a few inches. When you try to walk in this muck, you sink down to solid ice. Every step is a battle with the suction, as caked mud clings tighter and thicker onto your overshoes. It makes you feel as if each foot weighs twenty-five pounds.

Of all the problems I had to deal with, the most baffling one before I became a Christian was my constant habit of swearing. As a child I swore when I thought my father punished me unfairly. It was such a way of life with me, it was as if my feet were caked with the mud of profanity. It was also a way of life for people living in our logging camp, but swearing is not limited to any group of people today. You hear it in all walks of life and everywhere.

I knew swearing was not right and I was blaspheming God. When I swore, I was actually mad at him for what was happening to me. I blamed him. Long ago God had told Moses, "He that blasphemeth the name of the Lord shall be put to death" (Leviticus 24:16).

Habits are hard to break. Until the time I became a Christian I always thought you tapered off doing something you wanted to quit, little by little, day by day. You got better and better, and finally you stopped altogether committing a particular sin. Next you started on another weakness and concentrated until you overcame that one. I thought if you persevered long and hard enough, you'd get victory over any bad habit. I believed the only way to improve morally and spiritually was to have more willpower than you used before and to try harder.

When swearing was involved, however, this theory of getting better and better didn't work. Instead it failed completely.

One day while walking up a hill I was facing the sun and didn't notice a curving root winding across my path. Suddenly my toe caught and I tripped and sprawled spread-eagle on the ground.

As I stumbled and pitched forward I spoke aloud, "Dear God, please help me." Instead of swearing, I was praying. This time no oath boiled over inside me. Being a Christian was still new to me, but I was so in love with Jesus that I didn't want to do or say anything to dishonor his name. A few more such experiences proved, beyond the shadow of a doubt, that I was through with a lifetime habit: my profanity.

The fact that God instantly took away my inclination to swear has been a constant encouragement. It shows how great he is. It's proof to me that he can work in a person's life.

TWELVE
"Put Away Lying"

During my growing-up years I learned a lot about telling lies. I tried to be an expert at it and I succeeded fairly well. Telling a fib is often the easiest way to keep out of or get out of trouble. At the same time it can also be the simplest and quickest way to get further into trouble. I discovered that too.

There are many problems involved with telling lies. One is to try and remember what falsehood you told to which person. The situation can quickly get out of hand if two or more of your acquaintances get together and compare notes when you've told each one a prevarication of the same subject.

Why do people lie?

They tell lies because they're infected with the deadly poison of dishonesty. People deviate from truth because they don't want to face the reality of what is true. They alter facts to fit fancy. It's often a defense against shame. Much lying is criticism combined with boasting to try and achieve superiority. If you can't pretend to yourself by misrepresentation, you can outright falsify the truth.

With me at first it was a possible protection against being beaten. As a child the easiest way to defend myself was to fib. Of course, much of the time my lying didn't succeed in protecting me but I tried over and over again. Your mind is sharpened when you're trying to protect yourself. My two brothers and I could run as well as think. We talked fast when we needed to.

But my lying went far beyond our family circle. Because I was so poorly adjusted socially, I did everything I could think of to try and get my schoolmates and others to like me.

We moved so many times that, entering the third grade, I was in my sixth school. By then we'd settled in a town in Washington state. I was eight years old and small for my age, but after the first week in school the teachers decided I should be advanced to fourth grade. I was scared and the studies were harder. My third-grade friends rejected me and the fourth graders ignored me.

A day came when I hoped I could impress all the students in that room and get them to like me. A girl brought a bouquet of lilies of the valley. The teacher placed them on her desk for all to see. At recess I gathered a group of girls around me and told them that down in Texas our lilies of the valley grew taller than my head.

They scoffed, and I did my best to convince

them. "Only down in Texas we call them yuccas," I explained. "That must be their Spanish name."

They shrieked with laughter and one girl shouted, "Yuk, yuk, yuccas."

Then another little girl slipped away and ran in to tell the teacher what I'd said. In a moment the child exploded out of the building like a torpedo heading for its target. Behind her came the teacher and behind the teacher was the principal! These two grownups took long steps and I knew who they were aiming for.

One adult grabbed the sleeve of my dress and the other held onto my collar as they marched me into the principal's office. "We've had liars in this school before, but no one has ever made up such a story about lilies of the valley as tall as a man. Now to stay in this school, Ruth, you'll have to stop lying. You and your yuccas! Bah!"

That mental battering completely drained me of even a gram of self-worth. I slunk out of the principal's office, feeling small enough to crawl into a rat hole if I'd found one in that hallway.

Both the third and fourth graders were happy at my downfall. No one came near me all day. It was as if my face had been pushed in thick mud.

I kept on telling lies until my twelfth year when a kindly Camp Fire leader asked me to stay after the meeting. There she said simply, "Ruth, you're lying so much that when you speak we don't know what is true and what is false. This may get you into real trouble sometime. Don't you think it would be wise for you to stop?"

You can be sure I didn't thank her, but I did hide her words in my heart. I knew she was right, but I didn't stop because of its rightness. The thing that slowed my lying was that no one would believe me when I was honest. I'd be accused of untruth when I was trying to be sincere.

When I came to Jesus and knew I was born again into the family of God, I learned that Jesus is the way, the truth, and the life. I knew I had to do something about telling lies.

At this point I'd like to report that I stopped lying the way I quit swearing, but it didn't happen that way. I'm still tempted to lie when I need to get out of some predicament.

Recently such a problem came about and I kept still rather than let the blame fall where it belonged—on me. Arriving home afterward, I was still proud of myself that I had gotten by without anyone knowing about it. But that night I couldn't sleep.

The next morning I made some penitent phone calls. There was no peace ahead for me living a lie like that. I had to ask God's forgiveness and then make restitution by confession to others.

Nor did my problem with falsehood end with that. Sometime later I was discussing a business matter at the bank. At each question I answered truthfully until we came to a matter that was of great advantage to me if I said "yes." But the truth was "no." I said "yes." The discussion ended in a draw. Nothing was settled.

My sleep was unsettled that night. I kept asking myself, "When will you ever learn that even in the minutest details there's absolutely nothing to stretch? It's true or it's false."
I tossed and turned for what seemed like hours. I cried, "Dear God, please, please forgive me."

Then first thing in the morning I called the bank. I didn't try to whitewash it and say I'd made a mistake. Instead I told the girl I'd dealt with the day before, "I'm sorry, I lied yesterday."

She didn't embarrass me. She simply asked me to come in that afternoon again so we could finalize the matter.

Now here I am, trying to be a mature Christian, and within a year I've told two lies. I remember Peter and his denial of Jesus and I know that my lies are something of a denial too. I remember David and I hurry to read the 51st Psalm. I claim it as my own prayer in connection with my falsehoods.

The Bible states that lies are an abomination to the Lord. That means that God abhors lies. They are disgusting to him. A liar is in bad company, according to Proverbs, which lists what the Lord hates: a proud look, a lying tongue, and hands that shed innocent blood. That's pretty bad company—right next to a murderer. David prayed about lying: that it would be "put away" and he'd speak only truth with his neighbor.

Solomon, the wisest of all persons, said that he who hides hatred with lying lips and uttereth slander is a fool. I don't want to be a fool. The prophet Ezekiel was strong against lying when he wrote that lies make the heart of the righteous sad and strengthen the hands of the wicked. The apostle Paul said to put away lying and for everyone to speak truth with his neighbors.

With God's help, that's what I intend to do: speak the truth. The sin of lying is too big a burden for me to carry.

THIRTEEN
Fight Against Jealousy

Another serious problem began as jealousy. Jealousy is feeling inferior and seeing or believing that someone has something you should have but don't. Something you want but can't get.

Jealousy often develops into envy, a painful emotion of resentment with a wish to harm. The basis of envy is malice, with pleasure when misfortune or catastrophe comes to the prosperous rival.

My earliest remembrance of being jealous was when I was ten years old. A classmate and her father asked me to ride in their car. When this girl began to cough, her father was genuinely concerned. "Florence," he spoke gently, "I hoped your cold was over. Maybe you'd better stay inside this afternoon, away from the chill wind."

I was amazed. I could scarcely believe my ears. Imagine, her dad actually observed she had a cold and he was concerned. Further, on the way home he stopped at the drugstore and asked us what kind of ice cream cones we wanted. She didn't even ask or have to beg.

That night as I fell asleep I wished I had a dad like that. I begrudged her hers and wished I could trade my father for him.

That family was nice to me. They took me for a weekend vacation with them. But I was so jealous, I was ungrateful. Their kindness made me feel all the more inferior. We moved away soon.

A few years later when I was back visiting my aunts, Florence invited me to her home. After we'd talked about school she took me into her bedroom to show me her new clothes. Since she was an only child with adoring parents and relatives, she had oodles of pretty things. As she emptied her closet and piled her bed higher and higher with lovely garments, I began to feel inward rage at her for having so much when I had so little back at my house.

That day my feelings went beyond jealousy. I resented all she had and envied her. I believed she had everything. First was constant affection and devotion from her parents and relatives. She had a nicer home because her father was one of the company executives. She had many friends. At school she was popular with both boys and girls. She made good grades. The teachers adored her, and why not? Her father was on the school board.

Envy is a diabolical passion, which King Solomon called the rottenness of the bones (Proverbs 14:30). Saint Paul places envy next to murder (Romans 1:29). I felt a smoldering, persistent hope that something bad would happen to Florence, and soon!

Another person I envied was Sally, a classmate my senior year at Longview high school. She was such an excellent musician that she played the organ at her church and was paid for it. It was an unpardonable crime to me. I hadn't had the opportunities for training she had. We had no classes together, but one day when I passed her in the hall I thought it would be great if I could yell at her, "You think you're smart!" That was the strongest way I could say, "You're superior, I'm inferior." With my feelings of envy I was telling her, "Your ability to play so well makes me unhappy. You are the master of my feelings and I'm the slave, letting you control my emotions."

I was breeding contempt of myself. When I went off to college, I took all my heartburn of vulgar envy along with me. Time after time when I heard someone's high opinion of another person, I resented it. I'd try to tear down that other individual with my gossip.

My envy centered on Joan, who seemed to symbolize everything I wanted in life but couldn't get. She was three years ahead of me, so she left at the end of my freshman year. She was super in looks and charm and almost a concert violinist. As she drove away after graduation I thought, "The rich have everything, and I have nothing!"

She married an honor student the summer she graduated and she had twelve bridesmaids in her wedding party along with as many men. When I heard about it, I was all the more furious at her, seething with envy.

Even before I graduated, however, I changed my viewpoint entirely about Florence, Sally, and Joan. Their problems in later years were utterly crushing.

Florence was the first I learned about. When she went off to the university she pledged the top sorority on campus. When I heard that, I despised her. Then catastrophe struck. At the start of the second semester of her freshman year, Florence left school the morning after the sorority initiation. We soon learned the reason for her abrupt departure. Her father, the man I'd admired so much, had become an alcoholic. He was fired from his executive position. Florence, the girl who'd been pampered all her life, had to quit school to go home and stay with her aging parents.

Here was my chance to rejoice. I'd been wishing something terrible would happen to hurt her, and this had.

But I did a turnaround. Instead of feeling spiteful toward her and being glad, I was genuinely sorry for her sorrow and the sad change in her situation. I now felt deep compassion for the girl I'd envied for so long. I thought of all the years she and her mother must have tried to shield the father and keep people from finding out about him. How they hoped he'd change and he never did.

That next summer I met a friend and asked, "How is Sally?"

"She's back at Mayo Clinic again," was the answer.

I was instantly alert. "Why did she go there?"

"This is her second visit. You know Sally doesn't have a hair growing on her body. Back there they're trying everything to get her hair to grow again."

I was horrified. My rancor at Sally's success evaporated. Sally was bald. She wore a wig.

Bald? I felt faint at the thought. Here I'd been envious of her all this time, never dreaming she had such a great affliction in her life. I felt a wave of pity so strong I wondered how I could ever have been jealous or envious of her.

I didn't hear any more about Joan until my own commencement week. Someone had started talking about her and her brilliant husband. "Too bad about him."

"What's bad about such a handsome man?" I asked laughing.

"Why, he has a crippling disease and there's no remedy discovered yet. It will get progressively worse..."

My reaction to the news about Joan's grief was both compassion and pity, but it was more. I actually felt a concerned love for Joan and the distress she was facing.

Through the years, even with these and similar experiences, my fight against jealousy and envy has been difficult. Solomon said, "Wrath is cruel, and anger is outrageous; but who is able to stand before envy?" (Proverbs 27:4). Jealousy and envy wreck personal relationships in families, communities, schools, churches, organizations. This bad emotion makes havoc of people's getting along together in this world. The lasting solution to jealousy and envy is to rejoice in being part of the body of Christ. Just as the hand cannot feel superior to the foot, or the ear glory over the eye, each person has a part in the whole. Each one has his or her own function in the body of believers.

FOURTEEN
Answer to Gossip

It all started so quickly. The forked tongue of gossip attacked beautiful nineteen-year-old Gloria and she jumped to her death from a bridge. She left behind a terse message on a scrap of paper. The two words were, "They said..."

When police detectives tried to track down the unverified reports and slanderous lies, they were unable to pinpoint anything. No one accepted responsibility or admitted being at fault. It was too late anyway. Gloria was dead.

A suicide? Or killed by the poison of gossip?

The Bible says of gossips, "Adders' poison is under their lips" (Psalm 140:3). The word *gossip* was originally the Anglo-Saxon word *godsib*, which had a sacred and dignified meaning: "related to God." Next it came to mean idle talk and chatter. Now the general understanding of gossip is to repeat scandal. Yet gossip is easy to manufacture. Innuendoes lead to character assassination. To stop it is as futile as to try and pick up all the feathers of a pillow cut open and scattered in a brisk wind.

I learned to gossip from my mother, who was an expert. Together she and I practiced searching out the weaknesses of others. We downgraded and pulled people to pieces with careless tidbits. It was harmful and cruel, not mere idle chatter. Solomon identified a tale-bearer as one who reveals secrets: he says that one with a faithful spirit conceals a matter (Proverbs 11:13).

In my growing-up years, I believed that the quickest way to be liked and admired was to bring some news. The more shockingly I could tell it, the more popular I thought I'd be. I never imagined that others would like me better and feel safer with me if I defended someone now and then.

Gossip is like dry-rot. It shakes the basis of trust and confidence in friendships. When a person tells you an unsavory tale about someone else, you get the uneasy feeling that you may be the subject of the next conversation.

Gossip is like a forest fire because bad news always travels faster than good news. It voraciously devours good reputations. Gossip is like a flood. Afterward there's ruin and devastation and heartbreak. Gossip looks for the worst in everyone.

My mother felt that life had cheated her. It was almost a cruel hoax. I was angry at the wounds of my childhood and my rejection. Subconsciously I believed that if I pulled someone else down, I'd be equal to that one. I'd feel better about myself. If I could put someone below me for any shortcoming or lack or wrongdoing, then I'd be better. The trouble was it didn't work out that way. It just made me feel mean and confused and guilty. It confirmed the low opinion I had of myself.

My mother and I gossiped because we had no interest in things or concern for people outside ourselves. We went to church, but what we heard on Sunday had nothing to do with what we did the rest of the week. Once the young mother across the street from us was ill. She had small children and I suggested that we cook some food and take it over to her. I'd heard of people doing things like that and thought it was a good idea. My mother silenced me with the words, "She wouldn't bring me anything if I got sick."

So we did nothing. The poignant fact is that my mother did get sick the next winter after I was gone. People brought food to my parents, enough to last them for several days. That made a great impression on me.

In defense of my mother: with her hearing problem, it's true that she lived a lonely life. Gossip was her way of learning about people. It was the way she dealt with boredom.

After my "new birth," I had to deal with my criticism and faultfinding and evil words about others. "Every idle word that men speak, they shall give account thereof in the day of judgment" (Matthew 12:36). I knew I would be called into account for my gossiping, and

I resolved to stop. Giving it up was giving up an ego trip. There's nothing quite as satisfying as that astonished gasp when you tell someone a juicy morsel that person hadn't heard before.

I had a special moment when I first tried to stop some senseless babbling about another friend. I told the speaker, "I'm sorry you've had this bad experience. I know X quite well and I've found him above reproach. In fact, he thinks very highly of you and I'm surprised at what you're saying about him." I could scarcely believe my ears that I hadn't jumped in and helped run X down.

Another way to stop backbiting is to change the subject. Or to say nothing. Nothing is so deflating to a gossip as when the other person remains silent. It's like throwing pebbles into a well.

At other times the thing to do when vicious lies are being told is to defend the person being torn apart. "Pardon me, but I happen to know that what you're saying is not true. You are mistaken about your facts." Then you tell what you believe to be true.

Another way to solve cheap gabbing is to refuse to listen. The thing a gossip needs is an audience. When a downgrader starts in with, "It's hard to believe this about . . ." you can break in and say, "No, I'm not going to believe it because I don't want you to tell me about it. Let's talk about something else." It may be deflating to the other person, but it makes him or her think.

When the speaker insists, you can say, "I have

a tendency toward gossip—I'm asking God to help me overcome it and I'm asking you, for my sake, to change the subject."

Since I started walking with Jesus in newness of life, my gossiping has been the problem I've prayed about more than any other. I've grieved because I let myself be drawn into listening to hearsay and even slander about others. I've been a newsbearer when I should have concealed the matter from others. I have looked for failure in others.

But I've found one remedy that works better than any other. As the viciousness increases and the venom pours out against some person, I now try to remember to say, "I can see how concerned you are about this individual you're discussing" (dissecting would be a better description). "Now let's you and I go to see this other person and tell him [or her] your sentiments about how he [or she] is acting."

Or if this isn't possible I suggest, "Let's write down your complaint and we'll both sign it and mail it right now." "If a man is overtaken in a fault, you who are spiritual should restore him in a spirit of gentleness" (Galatians 6:1). It is amazing how quickly this will stop a deceitful tongue, the one that started out with, "Please, don't tell a soul, but ..." Maybe the reason for not telling was so the gossiper could be first to spread the bad news.

There is an antidote for gossip. The dictionary defines antidote as "a remedy to counteract the effects of a poison; whatever tends to prevent or counteract evil that something else might produce." The remedy is love. Love will protect someone instead of exposing him. Love will praise, commend, laud, and even glorify another. One of the most courageous and powerful things a person can do is to admit that someone else is better in any manner or endeavor than you are—and then to commend that person without trying to point out some flaw to criticize. That's hard. But it's love in action.

One great help to me has been a suggestion I heard about reading the Bible. I read two psalms each morning, then a chapter of Proverbs, and then two or more chapters from some other portion of the Scriptures. This way I have established a devotional pattern in my life.

On a visit to my parents' home, I didn't see any Bible in evidence, although I knew my mother owned one. During a conversation over a cup of tea and crumpets, my mother was vitriolic in her gossiping. Each person brought into the conversation was a baseball whom she batted with harsh words and judgmental criticism.

After an instant prayer for guidance, I asked my mother, "Do you read your Bible much?"

I was surprised at her answer. "No, I don't have to read it. I know lots about it and I know lots of what's in it."

I begged her to start studying it for herself and reluctantly she promised she would. My parents were still living in Ryderwood, and by then she had those thousand residents all psyched out. She knew every flaw and weakness of each one. She'd take generous cuds of a family's or a club's members and would chew on their shortcomings for as long as any listener would listen.

I didn't get back to see my mother until two years later, and by then a miracle had taken place in her life. Or rather, in her tongue. I had just arrived when a neighbor from across the street came over to say hello to me. After our greeting she turned to my mother and remarked, "That new lady next door to me doesn't wash her breadboard after she uses it. I was standing in her kitchen and I saw her pull it out all piled up with old flour and dough."

I waited, expecting my mother to pitch in and ask, "What else does she leave undone in her housekeeping?"

To my surprise, my mother started defending the new lady. "Anyone who bakes bread today with a family of three small children is to be commended, not condemned," she said matter-of-factly.

The gossiper left soon to carry her tale to someone more receptive and I hugged my mother. My heart brimmed with love and admiration for her. Reading the Bible faithfully had sweetened her tongue. Of the ideal woman in the Bible it is said, "The law of kindness is in her tongue" (Proverbs 31:26).

But there was another change in my mother's life. In the logging camps the men are usually young, since their work is strenuous. Since the families are young, they have babies, and people give showers. Somehow others could feel my mother's love emanating from within and soon she was invited to more showers in a year than many people attend in a lifetime. She loved going and enjoyed giving beautiful gifts. Further, anyone sick in that town probably received a large bowl of her superb tapioca pudding, along with a delicious cake. She's learned the joy of service and of giving.

My mother found the answer to gossip in the words of King David when he asked a question, "Lord, who shall dwell in thy holy hill?" The answer came, "He that walketh uprightly, and worketh righteousness and speaketh the truth in his heart. He that backbiteth not with his tongue" (Psalm 15:3).

That answer holds for us today.

FIFTEEN
Side Effects

Many of the "wounds" I suffered from others were not intentional. They were the sort of experiences everyone has in growing up. Some of my problems arose from my self-centeredness.

Other kinds of emotions churned inside me as I grew in my new life of faith. I sometimes felt like a giraffe, being five feet six inches tall. I towered over my mother, who was barely five feet in height. One brother was only five feet four inches. He had obviously taken after my mother. I took after my six-foot father. But I followed my mother's example in overeating and once weighed two hundred and five pounds. They don't make pretty girlish dresses in size forty-four, which I wore at that time.

It's difficult to sound convincing when as a new Christian you tell someone that, "God can do anything," and the hearer sees all the extra pounds you're carrying around. I was aware that I wasn't much of a testimony with the corpulence of my body, but I had another reason for losing weight. It hurt to walk because my heaviness was painful to the arches of my feet.

Folks who knew me before ask, "How did you take off all those excess pounds?"

My flippant answer often is, "By blood, sweat, and tears," and it is true. But it's not the most important part, because every pound that came off and stayed off is by the power of God. Otherwise I could easily and with great gusto and carnal enjoyment weigh three hundred pounds today. I've had to take seriously the admonition of King Solomon, "Put a knife to thy throat, if thou be a man [or a woman] given to appetite" (Proverbs 23:2).

Pride was another problem I had to face. And the need to straighten things out with others. I had to write letters asking pardon for some wrong I'd done to another. I had other wrongs to make right. My first letter was to a Whitmanite who'd been in one of my classes. In high school I'd sailed through advanced algebra and my father was determined I'd be a math major. In college, however, I just couldn't fathom calculus. I found a way out of my predicament. The girl who sat next to me was a math genius. She always had her lessons completed and almost always correct. So I'd fill out the problems on my paper each day, leaving plenty of space to copy down her answers while the teacher was talking and explaining everything. Being so busy copying, I learned nothing in class from our instructor.

I wonder yet why she let me do it. Of course it all ended when I flunked the final exam. I changed my major to economics, which used the kind of numbers I understood.

Soon after my new life with Christ began, I felt so ashamed of what I'd done in that class that I wrote this brilliant student a long letter, asking her forgiveness. I told her how much I appreciated her letting me copy and especially that she didn't report me to the professor. I told her I knew God had forgiven me and asked her if she would forgive me too.

My biggest problems remained where they'd always been: inside of me. I had a deep dissatisfaction and awareness that there was a vast chasm between what I really was as a Christian and what I believed God wanted me to be. I remember walking along a sidewalk and thinking, "If I don't get more of God, I'll simply die."

Soon after that I heard a speaker who ended his talk with, "If you want to mean business with God, raise your hand." I shot up my hand and was never more in earnest in my life.

Back at home my anger and bitterness still flared up when someone displeased me. About this time someone dear to me told me frankly, "You talk a lot about God, but you don't live the Life." That statement was a crushing blow. I was in an agony of despair. No matter how hard I tried, it was always the same. I needed more power to live the Christian life.

Ten days later someone invited me to go along to hear Peter Marshall, Jr., speak at an evening gathering. When it was over, my friend stood in a long line of people waiting for Peter to pray for them. I sat off by myself, sorry I'd come when I knew we'd be there a long time. Soon a man entered and said, "Anyone who wants to receive the Holy Spirit, come into the conference room."

Curious, I wandered in. I knew I'd received the Holy Spirit when I accepted Christ. But that night I found a new perspective in what Andrew Murray calls the Spirit's taking full possession of a person by pervading one's entire being. It was not my having more of the Holy Spirit, but the Spirit's having more of me.

I hadn't understood it before. I already knew that God wanted my dependence on him and my obedience. Now I realized that God wanted to fill my life with himself. He would work through me so that I could be the channel carrying his blessing to others. He had the power available.

I was aware of the presence of God in my life, but until that night I didn't understand that God was waiting to work through me. It was a totally new idea that I could pray to God the Father, through God the Son—and God the Holy Spirit would provide power in unfathomable supply. All I needed was to surrender all the aspects of my life that bound and incarcerated me. Then I could know the fullness of God's divine presence filling every nook and cranny of my being with his love, peace, and joy. Every muscle, every tissue, every bone.

With this new consciousness of the Holy Spirit at work in my life, I felt an anointing to be consecrated as a messenger of God's love. I asked God to take full possession of me and I had a new consciousness of Jesus Christ indwelling my life. I felt a sense of helplessness in myself, but a desire to give up the reign of self and put Christ on the throne of my life.

At the time when my spirit was crying out to God, I was like a dry, empty reservoir. And God filled me with the same Spirit which raised Jesus from the dead. I realize he wants to do his living through me: "Christ in you, the hope of glory" (Colossians 1:27).

My life as a child, battered in body, and as an adult, battered in spirit, was something like a big bucket clogged with dried leaves and twigs and dirt and dust. Then the love of Christ and the power of the Holy Spirit began to work in me as if a faucet were turned on. Pure, fresh water from God filled me and began to stir up the accumulation of debris. After a while a leaf would float out over the top and then particles of dirt or dust and then a few twigs would be washed over. Finally the water ran practically clean.

The only drawback was that down in the bottom of the bucket was a great big old brick. This represented a mass of guilt, hostility, and bitterness I felt toward those I thought had

wronged me. Talk about being inconsistent.
Here I was glorying in the fact that God had
forgiven me when I refused to forgive those I felt
had wronged me. I had tricked myself into
believing I could hold my grudges and my hopes
for revenge. That I could ignore the phrase
in the Lord's prayer, "Forgive us our debts as we
forgive our debtors—or, as in another rendition,
"Forgive us our trespasses as we forgive those
who trespass against us."

I'd never learned consideration of anyone
besides myself, so I didn't ever look at my
relationships from other people's point of view.
As a result I had a problem with guilt. I felt
guilty because I was ashamed of my home
situation. Once in a while I wished I'd been born
a boy because I believed if I'd been male, I'd
have fitted better into our family life. Especially
I wished that if I had to be a girl, I'd have been
pretty.

But my greatest problem concerned my father
and my attitude toward him. I felt ashamed
when he berated me, but I also felt guilty because
I couldn't do better and please him more.
I regretted that sometimes I was the one who
made him so mad he acted like a furious monster
toward one of us children.

One day when I was feeling unusually sorry, I
decided to write down all the people and
places I could remember where I'd been hurt, and
who and how anyone had hurt me.

I started scribbling the places first. Experts tell
us that there are hidden recesses in our sub-
conscious where every incident of a lifetime is

stored away, including all the wounds of childhood. In this vast depository every criticism, all berating and fault-finding, every tongue-lashing and emotional abuse are filed away. This is a possible explanation why someone immediately takes a dislike to a person never seen before. It may be a link back to someone who was hated in childhood. The animosity is transferred to this newly met man or woman. I'm sure this is why sometimes in the past I've had an instant aversion toward some man. It's because this stranger reminds me of my father, whether by looks, words, or manner.

After I'd listed all the places, I started to write down people whom I resented, detested, loathed, or outright hated. I opened doors I'd bolted tightly shut in my thought-rooms, locked from anyone else's eyes. There were secret closets and cupboards and hidden corners that hadn't been opened since early childhood. My father's name came first. I listed all the heartbreak he'd caused our family. The rougher he was to us children, the more it bothered me, but also the greater my guilt. My underlying rage at my mistreatment was because I thought my dad was totally unfair to his wife, my mother, and to us youngsters. I realized that the brutality of his stepfather had been all the worse to him because he'd been his own father's favorite. The shock of this experience had affected his entire life and he had never recovered from the hurt of it.

Just before his second and fatal heart attack,

my father kept writing to me, asking in his letters, "Do you think God could ever forgive me for the life I lived and the way I treated all of you?"

I always answered "yes," but I myself wasn't doing any forgiving. I still held resentment and bitterness toward him.

Since God doesn't close his accounts until after the last heartbeat, I believe that after the anguish and regret of my dad's later life, God forgave him and that he's now in heaven.

The second name on my list surprised me. It was my mother.

Until the moment when I penned her name I wasn't conscious that I held a grudge against her. I'd felt so sympathetic toward her that I didn't realize I was bitter toward her at the same time. I resented my mother's attitude toward having guests in our home. I thought she used her difficulty in hearing as an excuse for not entertaining.

I believed that much of my trouble arose from my not being equipped to meet life. In the Bible the prophet Samuel was judged because it was said of him concerning his evil sons, "He restrained them not" (1 Samuel 3:13).

My mother never hurt anyone knowingly, but she never taught me regard for others. She knew how to conduct herself on all occasions and in all circumstances, but she didn't teach me how to behave or take account of my manners. As a result I grew up a logging camp boor. She never made me turn my hand at housework, although after we left the South she had to do it all herself. I had to learn it all the hard way, later and alone.

But my mother gave me a priceless heritage.

While I was visiting her after my dad's first heart attack, she asked me, "What's going to become of me when Dad goes?"

I was living in Los Angeles at that time and she was in Washington state.

"I'll come and get you that very day and you'll live with me," I assured her.

"Well, Ruth," she smiled as she said the words I'll never forget, "it'll only be a little while..."

Six weeks later my father had recovered enough that he planned to go on a fifty-mile errand early the next morning. "Don't leave without waking me," my mother asked him. When he seemed reluctant to call her, she made him promise to wake her.

As the faint light of day dawned, my father dressed silently and then reached across to touch my mother. She did not respond. She had died in her sleep.

Whether she had a premonition the night before we don't know. But I do know that her words, "It'll only be a little while..." have been a blessing to me when things are complex or I feel depressed. I know that God is with me and that no matter how many long years there are yet ahead of me on this earth, it will be "only a little while" until I see her again in heaven.

Remembering all this, I wept. It was a deeply emotional experience to search among all the unhappy memories stored in my mind. On and on the list grew. In spite of the sadness, I kept on digging up the grief.

When I finished my long list, I went away by myself on a vacation to face the issue of these grievances and all the ways I believed life had wronged me.

Of course the most difficult of all to forgive was my father. My dad often wasted his money in riotous living. But I did a resume of my father and to be honest I had to admit that he stood behind me financially when I wanted an education. He always came back to us after his many affairs. He'd never been drunk. It was a sobering thought to realize how loyal he'd been in spite of everything else amiss.

If at times he felt any tenderness toward us, we never encouraged him in it. We didn't expect any kindness from him and weren't ready to receive it if he'd tried to show it.

Even when we went to the same places, my dad never walked or sat with us. When we came home, he always hurried ahead and was either reading the paper or fussing around in the house or outside by the time we arrived. Perhaps he was trying to escape our hostility all those years.

He'd turned his back on God who could have helped him when he finally admitted his inadequacies.

I'd already asked God to forgive my father when he wrote me the desperate letters. Now it was my turn to forgive.

I mulled all this over in my mind and then I

remembered something else. We hear so much about incest these days. I'm so thankful that my father never molested me. It could have been worse.

My bottled-up feelings toward him gradually drained away. The ugliness and sordidness evaporated under the sunshine of God's forgiveness, through me toward him.

Suddenly I felt warmth and a heavenly sorrow that he was gone and I couldn't tell him I loved him. But with it was a quiet joy and assurance that my father knows how I feel and how much I love him now.

It wasn't a big deal to forgive my mother, when I hadn't even been aware I held anything against her. By being too easy on me she was trying to make it up to us children because of a father who was too hard on us. In her gentleness she was a benediction on my life. I don't recall that she ever yelled at me, and I was the kind who needed correction. I'm sorry that neither of us knew how to bridge the communication gap between us. As a result we left much unsaid, words of appreciation and affirming each other and praising where praise was due.

With my list before me, I prayed separately for each person and every situation. It took a long time and I asked God to take away all the grief and distress and unhappiness and sadness and sorrow. I had to keep stopping along the way to acknowledge and accept any responsibilities for my mistakes of judgment or action in anything. Then I had to ask God to forgive the people I mentioned, just as I expected God to forgive me for my imperfections and sins of omission and commission.

Relief did not come all at once. I had to return over and over again to some names and places. But even if it was slow, healing came. Habits are hard to break. My habit of blaming my mother for some of my troubles was my way of evading my own responsibility for some of my actions.

As I look back on my mother's life, I believe that she evidenced the most sacrificial love I could imagine. One son was taken from her when he was five years old. Next my mother sent me away when I was sixteen years old to another high school. The Bible says, "Greater love hath no man than this, that a man lay down his life for his friends" (John 15:13). I can paraphrase that verse to express what my mother did: "Greater love hath no mother than this, that she send away her eldest son and her only daughter for their safety and successful progress in life." That's what she did for Frank and me.

Any other aspects that she missed in my training are as nothing compared to this sublime manifestation of her love. Now I'm so ashamed that I held a grudge against her. There was nothing to forgive. I love her with all my heart, and am so grateful to her.

I kept on to the end of all the pages. When I finished, I felt as if God had taken me in his arms and helped me along. Or even carried me, the way I'd always wished my father had done. In my

spirit I knew what it must have been like
to be in a garden with God as Adam and Eve
were when they walked and talked with him in
the cool of the evening.

Christian counselors could have helped me.
Psychotherapy and deep therapy could have
aided and hurried my healing. I wish I'd had
those helps, but through my experiences God has
revealed himself to me in redemption through
Jesus. I know the power of his resurrection
and the fellowship of his sufferings. I've learned
to count on the abiding presence and fullness
of the Holy Spirit. For all of this I give thanks.

I am no longer a battered child. Many of the
pieces of my life puzzle now fit together. I can
rest in the comfort that I don't have to worry
about what I don't understand. I know I belong to
a loving, all-powerful heavenly Father. I'm
not so wistful anymore.

Yes, it's taken a long time. But at last I accept
the fact that I'm unique, irreplaceable, and
incomparable because God made me. Whatever
God has for me in the future, I want to be where
he wants me. I am in God's presence whether
living here on earth or what we call dead—
which means that I'll be in his presence
eternally. I'll be with him forever, a Beloved
Daughter.

Epilogue

When I was twenty-two years old, I met a young student at the seminary, Edward Baird, whose life was a welcome contrast to mine. A graduate of Washington and Jefferson College in Pennsylvania, he was gracious, poised, and kindly. He didn't seem to care that I was plain and somewhat awkward. We just liked each other.

Then we fell in love, and I knew that wherever Edward went, I wanted to go. His people would be my people. We already had the same God. We were married on graduation day. After a lifetime of feeling left out, snubbed, and rejected, I suddenly became a beloved wife–a minister's wife. It was the second greatest day of my life.

Not long ago I told Edward, "Some other girl might have been a better wife to you, but no one could have loved you more," and he replied, "I'll settle for that!"

For me, marrying him was like stepping into heaven.

But our first pastorate was not heaven for either of us. I didn't know much about churches. I was completely ignorant about elders, stewards, deacons, trustees, let alone congregational meetings. But I soon learned. I learned also that people expected so much of me!

After a couple of months I started begging Edward to go back to teaching. He'd taught one year before entering seminary. He'd answer patiently, "But God called me to preach."

I needed help, and after six months, God sent me help in a friend, a young doctor's wife. I poured out to her how I didn't like being a minister's wife and how I wanted Edward to return to teaching.

She listened, then she told me the story of how her teacher-husband had wanted to be a doctor and how they had struggled to get him through medical school. "You have to let your husband do what he wants and be a good wife to him," she said.

Those were bitter words to hear, but I tried to take her advice and do what my husband wanted me to do in the church.

When our first child was on the way, I felt deeply honored that God would trust us with a fragile gem of humanity to raise for him. Tirzah's birthday was the third greatest day of my life.

Later we moved to a larger church, and there we had two more little girls, Ginger and Esther.

I shall be eternally grateful for the friends

God sent along my way. A special one was Aunt Addie, a missionary. One morning I saw her yawning and asked why she was sleepy. She said she'd been up since four A.M., praying for four hundred Chinese Christians she'd left behind in China.

In our third pastorate there was no Aunt Addie, so I made my own prayer list and started praying. One special answer to those prayers was our son, Forrest.

I'm astonished at what God has done for me. How good he was, to take a frightened girl who was bruised, hurt, and lonely for twenty-two years and give her peace and joy. In deep thankfulness I give God the glory for what he has done in my life.

If God did all this for me, he can do it for anyone.

LIVING BOOKS

*Inspirational bestsellers from the people
who brought you The Living Bible.*

WHAT WIVES WISH HUSBANDS KNEW ABOUT WOMEN by Dr. James Dobson. By the best-selling author of *Dare to Discipline* and *The Strong-Willed Child*, here's a vital book that speaks to the unique emotional needs and aspirations of today's woman. An immensely practical, interesting guide. #07 7896, $2.50

SLIM LIVING DAY BY DAY by JoAnn Ploeger. The official book of the YMCA's Slim Living Program. It contains the same wit, wisdom, and inspiration which has made the Slim Living program work in hundreds of cities and thousands of lives. #07 5913, $2.25.

BEYOND STAR WARS by William F. Dankenbring. The Exodus . . . Noah's flood . . . the great pyramid . . . Joshua's longest day . . . Atlantis . . . what really happened? Here's the real story of star wars, of battles in the universe. #07 0143, $2.50

HANSI by Maria Hirschmann. A different type of WW II story—one you won't forget. Escape, romance, and a new life in America are the highlights of this bestseller. #07 1294, $2.50.

HOW TO BE HAPPY THOUGH MARRIED by Dr. Tim LaHaye. One of America's most successful marriage counselors gives practical, proven advice for marital happiness. #07 1499, (October release). $2.25.

AMERICA AT THE CROSSROADS by John Price. America can escape national decline, economic collapse, and devastating conflict. But she must change her direction: she is now at the crossroads. #07 0064, (October release). $2.50.

REACH OUT. For the first time ever the New Testament from *The Living Bible* is available in a handy inexpensive pocket paper size. More than 30 million copies so far! #07 5206, (November release). $2.95.

ELIJAH by William H. Stephens. A rough hewn farmer who strolled onto the stage of history to deliver warnings to Ahab the king and to defy Jezebel the queen. A powerful biblical novel you will never forget. #07 4023, (November release). $2.50.

HINDS' FEET ON HIGH PLACES by Hannah Hurnard. A classic allegory which has sold more than a million copies! #07 1429, (December release). $2.95.

THE BRIDE'S ESCAPE by Donita Dyer. A breathtaking romance featuring escape, intrigue, and excitement. It's the story of Pearl, whose love touched two worlds. #07 4812, (December release). $2.50.

SEARCH FOR THE TWELVE APOSTLES by William Steuart McBirnie. What really happened to the original disciples of Jesus? The author, a Bible scholar and television personality, has uncovered the history of the apostles and their activities after Christ's death. A dramatic tale of men of courage and dedication. #07 5839, (January release). $2.50.

SOMEBODY LOVE ME by Jan Markell. Sick of herself and her problems, Sandy cried out for the ultimate high she had never known. A Living Books original true story. #07 6065, (January release). $2.25.

ORDER FROM YOUR BOOKSTORE.

If your bookstore does not stock these titles, order from:
LIVING BOOKS
Tyndale House Publishers
336 Gundersen Drive
Wheaton, Illinois 60187

Please send me the books indicated. Enclosed is my payment plus 25¢ per copy to cover postage and handling. Illinois state residents add applicable sales tax.

NAME _____

ADDRESS _____

CITY_____STATE_____ZIP_____

Amount Enclosed_____Cash_____Check_____Money Order_____(No. C.O.D s)

SPECIAL OFFER:

If you enjoyed this book and would like to have a listing of other inspirational books plus a complete listing of Living Bibles available from Tyndale House, just send your name and address and 50¢ (to help defray postage and handling costs) to: Catalog department, Tyndale House Publishers, 336 Gundersen Drive, Wheaton, Illinois 60187.